VISION TO REALITY
How Short Term Massive Action Equals
Long Term Maximum Results

By: Honorée Corder

Published by Honorée Enterprises Publishing, LLC.

Copyright 2014 ©Honorée Enterprises Publishing, LLC
& Honorée Corder

ISBN: 978-0-9847967-8-6

Discover other titles by Honorée Corder at
http://www.HonoreeCorder.com, Amazon.com,
BarnesandNoble.com, Smashwords.com and on
iBooks.

Table of Contents

VISION TO REALITY

Foreword

To say that Honorée Corder is a student of personal and professional development would be inaccurate. In fact, it's more like, if a PhD were available, she would qualify many times over. And, to say that Honorée Corder isn't interested in results would be more inaccurate still; if she were a character in a movie she would be Cuba Gooding Jr. from 'Jerry Maguire' shouting, "Show me the money!" And so it's not surprising with a background and beliefs like this, that she was inspired to write her latest book, *Vision to Reality*.

We were fortunate enough to meet Honorée at a conference several years ago and she was kind enough to read our book and provide us with feedback. As a result, she has been a cheerleader, mastermind partner, butt-kicker, and good friend ever since. So writing this foreword has provided us with the opportunity to sing her praises, because the method that she teaches in this book has been successful with client after client, year after year.

In short, Honorée is into getting results – big results – and getting them fast. You will be guided through Honorée's foundational concepts including vision, goals, focus, and relationships and then introduced to the process Honorée has pioneered, something she calls: STMA. It is a powerful, 100-day program that provides anyone who is willing to apply themselves with "Short Term Massive Action." What you'll find yourself thinking along the way is how simple the plan is. That's exactly the point. Of course, if you're like most people, you'll find yourself tempted to complicate it. Don't! It's perfect the way it is.

We've personally gone through the process and can say that if you work it as Honorée has laid it out, you will have a clear roadmap to achieving your short-term goals. Of course, short-term goals are stepping-stones on the path to long-term maximum results and the life you've always dreamt of. And for Honorée, that is what it is all about; taking you from your vision - whatever it may be - to the reality you deserve!

Richard Fenton & Andrea Waltz
Authors, *Go for No!*

Dear Reader:

Welcome to *Vision to Reality,* I'm delighted you're here! If you, like most of my coaching clients, are ready to break through to new levels of balance, success and fulfillment, you're holding the right book. As an executive and business coach for the past fifteen years, I see fantastic professionals struggle with going to the next level, while balancing family, their time, and their personal interests. I've cracked the code on creating success, and this book outlines what I've discovered.

The STMA (Short Term Massive Action) 100-day Coaching Program, in its original form, was designed in the early '90s for one person: me. Little did I know then that coaching and training were going to become my life's work ... I just wanted to reach my own personal and professional goals, and I wanted to reach them as quickly and easily as possible.

Laziness? Perhaps, and I prefer to call it *strategic,* maybe even *efficient.*

In search of what worked best, fastest, and easiest, I listened to thousands of hours of cassette tapes, went to seminar after seminar, and read book after book. Eventually, I developed a system that worked great for me, one that kept me on track and made reaching my goals a lot simpler and definitely easier.

Now, almost twenty years later, that original system, which I now call "STMA" is one of my most popular coaching programs. Using my Five Points of Accountability System™, you are set up to win and virtually protected from failure. In fact, the only way to fail *is to quit.* In a word: don't.

Vision to Reality was originally written as the companion book to the STMA Coaching Program, which was specifically designed to get you – and keep you -- going in the right direction. You can read it and use some or all of the elements in here to maximize everything from your overall happiness to the career success you desire. You can use it on your own, or with the additional accountability coaching provides. However you choose to move forward, with the power combination of your commitment, coaching, the additional structure of the Program, and your personal determination, **you are unstoppable**. You are, as of this very instant, moving toward your Big Hairy Audacious Goals. You are about to make your Vision your real Reality.

Are you ready? Let's go!

To your best success!

Honorée Corder
Visionary, Strategist, Writer, Coach, Wife, Mom

Chapter One:
What Do You Really Want and Why Haven't You Already Got It?

"Accountability is the mother of accomplishment."
~Honorée Corder

The alarm goes off at 5 a.m. Ted reaches over and presses snooze for the first of six or seven times. He knows he can sleep until just after 6:15 a.m. and still have enough time to make it to the office in time for the mandatory staff meeting. The passion has long ago left him, but he knows if he stops working, eventually he and his family will live in their minivan, at least until it's repossessed by the bank. He drags himself out of bed, grumbling all the while, as he gets ready for another day, *hopeful* he will be successful yet full of doubt and uncertainty.

Ted's day, like most of his days, consists of endless meetings, emails, and phone calls. Sometimes he meets a buddy for lunch, and almost every night of the week he's out networking, always hoping he's going to meet *that one guy* who's going to give him the deal to make his year. His networking events are chosen based on who invites him to this or that event. In fact, living in reaction instead of being proactive is how Ted does just about everything – by the seat of his pants, *hoping* success will cross his path.

5

What's wrong with this picture? I know, besides everything? Ted lacks the analysis, intention, planning, and action required to achieve his goals. By adding in these elements, he could more than make his yearly goals by May, year after year. Simple, easy-to-execute shifts in his thinking and behavior could yield results many times greater than what he's currently producing, and in, dare I say, less than half the time or maybe even in less than a third of the time. Imagine having all of your work completed by mid-morning on Wednesday. What would you ever do with yourself? What could you do with extra time: reach bigger goals? Bring a dream to fruition? Travel? Learn languages? Start new ventures? The list is endless.

If you're resonating a little too much with ole Ted right now, then you've picked up the right book. No more living a life of quiet desperation. No more wishing, and hoping, and settling. Not one more day.

No matter how long you've been in your current business, profession, or career, if you haven't reached your definition of the pinnacle of success, it can only mean one of two things: you haven't been in business long enough, or you haven't discovered the -- *your* -- personal success system that will create and continue to create the results you want.

The good news is you have at your fingertips that very system: the STMA. If, up until now, the success you've achieved has been through some good luck[1] combined intuition and some fairly decent choices, then you're in for a treat. I've got some great news for you, and it starts with the fact that you've managed to get this far, and you've done it most likely without being intentional, strategic, and consistent. What you've got here is a recipe that will help you to discover what can happen when you *are* intentional, strategic and consistent.

What's the STMA?

The STMA, which stands for *Short Term Massive Action*, is a personal and professional achievement system I developed to ensure my personal success. Once I'd road-tested it for several years {ahem, a decade}, I started using it in my one-on-one, and eventually my group, coaching practice.

I looked at successful people and had no idea how exactly they created their success. I listened to Tony Robbins, went to his seminars, even did the fire walk {it was awesome!}. I attended several other seminars, read hundreds of books, and listened to thousands of hours of success audios. Eventually I figured out there were several common characteristics, behaviors and beliefs successful people had that unsuccessful people didn't. I figured if I wanted to be successful, I needed to figure out the best way to integrate them all into my life and business, and do it as quickly as I could. Like yesterday.

---

[1] My definition of Good Luck is "preparation meets opportunity."

The STMA was the structure I put together for myself based upon what I saw the successful people I admired doing. I knew I needed a plan that included a vision, purpose, and goals, and also other elements to keep me focused and on track. I worked at it for a couple of years defining, refining, retooling, and reshaping until I figured out a simple yet effective system that doubled my income again and again, and allowed me to work only 6-7 hours a day. As a single mom, that was not just a desire, it was a necessity. My STMA was so effective for me that I started achieving my normal annual goals in the space of 100 days, or less.

I found that if I gave myself a year to achieve my goals, I would not feel any urgency to actually begin to take action. After all, a year is *forever*. The goals themselves would be big, but in and of themselves, that wasn't enough for me to take consistent action. Setting monthly goals didn't work for me either. Thirty days went by fast, and goals I set would be too big to achieve in such a short time. I would be disappointed in my performance, and beat myself up when I didn't reach them. I eventually settled on 100 days, and you'll read more about that later. It turns out 100 days was the perfect amount of time for me to achieve significant goals because I had enough time, but not too much time. Not too short, not too long … *just right.*

The STMA itself is simple and we're going to cover all of the elements of designing a successful 100 days for you. In fact, you can read all about the STMA and options you have for participating in it if you'd like at the end of the book. But first, let's focus just on you and determine what you need next-most in order to achieve everything you want out of life.

What's the Gap?

You would most likely take on the STMA, or engage in any type of coaching process, because there's a gap you'd like to close – you want to make more money, double your sales, start a new business, have more assets under management, or more new originations (that others in your firm work on), or find many additional clients or customers, and you want any and all of those things without all of the stress, long hours, and time away from your family. Chet Holmes, author of *The Ultimate Sales Machine*, said *"Success isn't doing twelve million things; it's doing a few things twelve million times."*

He's right: there are certain actions, when done constantly and consistently, that cause crucial results to occur. Among them, you become more effective and efficient, you get results faster, you stop doing the things that don't work, and you have more time to do more of the things you do want to do. The bonus is that these actions then become *habits.* Habits are what we're going for, but it's too soon to talk about them. So, hang on to your hat and keep reading.

You're not achieving your goals, in part, because you haven't been laser-focused and doing what works effectively every single time you do it. In addition, lack of achievement and/or accomplishment means there's lack of accountability and lack of systems that support success. It's too easy to let yourself off the hook.

You can make excuses all day long about how it's too cold, too late, you're too tired, you don't have enough money, you're too tall, too short, over-educated, or under-qualified … oh, that list just wore me plum out … to do what you say you want to do. You can have the best ideas in the world, you can wake up full of vim and vigor, but the minute something gets in your way, you let yourself slide. Don't you?

Come on, it's an extremely rare person who will jump out of bed first thing in the morning, complete his to do list by noon, say "no" to the cheesecake, complete his workout, read instead of watching television, make the calls he needs to make, answer all of his emails in a reasonable amount of time … all without knowing that someone (or many someones) is going to ask whether the actions that cause success are getting done. Just doesn't happen.

You know where your gaps are, and you know what you want out of your life and business, specifically in the next 100 days, and in the coming months and years. Before we get into the "how," let's talk about the "who."

Who Do You Need to Be?

Let me start off by saying you don't "need" to be anything. I am going to share with you what would be most effective for you to do to be successful, should you decide to opt in. What I believe is equally as important as what you're "doing" is who you are "being." Meaning, how good does it feel to be around you, to do business with you? Do you make it comfortable for others to be in your presence, or are they less than at-ease or even uncomfortable when they see you? It does not go without saying that some people make creating success easier on themselves by being a person of certain qualities and characteristics, and some people just don't. Some people are easy and fun to be around, some people are cranky, grumpy, and toxic. Which are you?

Who you need to be is as simple as this: You can make even double the right amount of calls. You can follow-up consistently for years. You can even be a gifted technician in your area of expertise. You can do everything "right," but if others don't like you, they won't do business with you unless they absolutely have to. Most of the time, no one absolutely *has* to do business with you. They don't have to, they won't, and they will tell others to avoid you like the black plague.

You can lose everything you gain through hard work and dedication if you don't have the qualities and characteristics to maintain and sustain it. Who you are "be-ing" is just as important, if not more important, then anything and everything you are "do-ing."

If for some reason you're the person people avoid, then prior to starting any goal-getting pilgrimage, you must spend a measureable amount of time turning yourself into a positive-thinking, good-feeling inducing, all-around fun person like your livelihood depends on it … because it does.

You'll probably need some tangibles to get you started, and here they are:

There are the four key cornerstones of a successful person: *talent, character, attitude*, and *skills*. With

11

one exception, the skills piece, each of the other three centers around what you've been given naturally, what you choose to do, and who you choose to be. It's these three that require undivided focus and attention, lest we work hard to create something only to have it come undone because of our personality and personal choices.

Talent. A natural aptitude for what you do means you'll be good at it, and you'll really like to do it. In fact, the more you like to do something, the more you do it and the better you get at it. This is both for things you like to do, and for things you don't care to do. Just because you *can* do something, doesn't mean you want to do it or like to do it. A skill is actually an ability to perform a task. Having natural talent for something means you have an almost instinctive and intuitive ability to do something, and we can all agree the things that come easiest to us are the things we most enjoy doing.

> Calvin Coolidge said about talent, *"Nothing in this world can take the place of persistence. Talent will not; nothing is more common than unsuccessful people with talent. Genius will not; unrewarded genius is almost a proverb. Education will not; the world is full of educated failures. Persistence and determination alone are omnipotent."*

Clearly talent is not enough, but it adds a critical ingredient to the mix. I love working with professionals who have found the work they love and can't wait to get into the office each day. Many times they love turning their big idea into a big company, writing a complex estate plan, or completing a tax return, only to discover that the amount of administrative tasks and other professional responsibilities detract from the amount of actual work they get to do. Soon, they are dissatisfied with the path they've taken and are thrilled to discover through our work how to cross those items off of their to do list faster and easier (many times through delegating), so they can get back to doing what they love to do. Truly, when you do what you love, money, success, and happiness are sure to follow.

Coach's Note: The more you love what you do, the more you will love your life. There's a direct correlation between someone who loves life because they are using their innate talents, and someone who is fun to be around. You see what I did there?

Character. I believe in order to be successful it's vital to be a dependable, reliable person others can count on to do what you say you are going to do, and do it when you say you are going to do it {or before}. The qualities of integrity, good moral character, and being ethical breed an environment of trust, and trust could be considered a strong contender for the top cornerstone of success. I personally have an automatic basic trust level with all people. It's up to them whether they increase or decrease my trust through their words and actions.

Abraham Lincoln said,
"Reputation is the shadow.
Character is the tree."

Our character is much more than just what we try to display for others to see; it is who we are even when no one is watching. Good character is doing the right thing because it is the right thing to do. Period.

I've noticed people can sense the characters of others, even without a lot of exposure to them, their actions or even words. We sense things about people, even if we can't explain what we're feeling. Make no mistake, if your character and what you portray your character to be are incongruent, others will know it!

I recently had a client who made a payment more than two weeks after it was due. Then, the check was returned for insufficient funds, complete with a fee from my bank. Phone calls and emails remain unanswered and unreturned. Now there's no trust in the relationship, and I could never hire or refer this professional based upon this experience.

Alternatively, another client sent me the following email a full ten days before her payment was due:

> *Hey Coach, I've got several deals in the pipeline, but with personal and corporate taxes, and other unexpected expenses, I would prefer to not use my debit card for this month's payment. Could I call you to provide you with a credit card instead? Thank you! ~Your Grateful Client*

Of course, this simple note not only left the state of our relationship intact, it actually enhanced it on many levels. Even if she had said, "I need more time to make my payment," that would have been fine. Every single professional, to a person, is amenable to someone who is up front about any and every situation and communicates with integrity.

14

Whether you're running ten minutes late to a meeting, or you are going to take longer to deliver a product or service, communication where you take 100% responsibility is a key factor in a successful relationship.

Isn't business made up of relationships? I say, "Yes, it is." I've heard the saying, "It's not personal, it's business," and so have you. I disagree, however, because I don't think there's anything more personal than business because I believe, in fact, that the best business is most personal.

Benjamin Franklin designed for himself a plan for building character that certainly seems to have been successful in many respects. He identified thirteen character qualities that he felt he needed to improve in his own life, and he devised a method of focusing his attention on each of those qualities for one week at a time. During a year's time, Mr. Franklin would go through his entire list four times.

A major part of having a solid character is to hold to your agreements, and in the event circumstances change and you cannot uphold your agreement, *you must make a new, mutually agreed upon arrangement.* This strategy applies to every single possible commitment or arrangement, including being on time, paying on time, fulfilling the details of a contract, or even making a promised introduction. You, like Benjamin Franklin, can determine the traits you want to develop. There's always another level, and self-improvement through character focus is no exception. What first becomes an action item, with attention and accountability, eventually becomes a habit.

Coach's Note: When you have a solid character, you're able to be carefree for the simple fact you're not doing anything you wouldn't want your spouse, boss, employees, or the *New York Times* to find out about. You give your word, you keep it, it's good, and so are you. See how those dots connect? Pretty cool, right?

Attitude. People are attracted to other people who "feel good" to them. The people you most likely feel great around are the people who are easy to be with, who make you feel good about yourself, and who encourage you to be your best self. This "beingness" creates a positive environment in which you can excel.

Without question, one of the most important elements in determining one's success is his or her attitude. I've noticed it's really easy to have a great attitude when things are going great. What about when you're experiencing challenges? Your potentially positive attitude comes from controlling your mental real estate: your most valuable property is that which lies between your two ears.

When you're on top of the world, it seems as though everything goes right. This state of flow can be attributed to "like attracts like." You may have heard the saying, "The best time to close a deal is when you've just closed a deal." You've reached a high vibration or have gotten in a flow state that seemingly makes things happen. The opposite also seems to be true: you lose a client, then another, and then another. What you're focusing on, you're getting ... positive or negative.

If you want to begin to or continue to "trend up," here are five excellent action steps to get you started:

- Remember, "be, do, and have." You must *be* positive and then *do* the right things to *have* (get) what you want. To be enthusiastic, you must decide to be enthusiastic and fake it 'til you make it.

- Shift and the world shifts with you. Decide today is going to be an awesome day. Expect it to be awesome. Sit in a field of positive expectation and wonder what great thing is going to happen next.

- When something less-than-fantastic happens, you can respond or react. Choose to respond in whatever way is appropriate and then press the reset button on your attitude.

- Dedicate yourself daily (hourly if necessary) to expanding the scope of your positive attitude.

- Daily: Think positive. Read positive. Listen positive. Talk positive. Affirm positive. Watch positive. Practice positive. *Make yourself positive.*

To ensure your beingness and attitude are at their best, I suggest you read *The Miracle Morning* by Hal Elrod. Hal emphasizes the importance of a morning routine that sets you up for success each and every day. Left to chance, perhaps you will have a good day, perhaps not. By creating a morning routine, you can set the odds heavily in your favor of having an epically fabulous day. Why not increase the odds you will have a fantastic day, full of energy, hope and enthusiasm?

Success starts with attitude. Make sure yours is positive, expectant, upbeat, and infectious … and pretty much at all times.

What success in life all boils down to is that it is "who you be" that factors more heavily into your success than "what you do." Keep a keen eye on your being-ness, and you will find it easier to do the things you know you need to do, and as a result amazing things will show up in your life and business.

> *"Thinking you can achieve something unleashes the force that allows it to happen."* ~Honorée Corder

Chapter Two:
What IS Possible?

*"Anything is possible when you believe you can,
have a plan and take consistent, persistent, and
intentional action toward its attainment."*
~Honorée Corder

As high achievers know, your beliefs are crucial to your success. Here's a truth for you: The possibilities are endless. Not just for others, for *you*. What you can achieve is most likely much, much bigger and more awesome than what you may believe right now you can achieve. What we can achieve and what we do achieve is so incredibly often miles and miles apart. In my coaching practice, I *daily* see people with amazing potential that has yet to be reached. What's preventing them from major victory, unlimited abundance, and massive success? Most of the time it is the story they have created about how getting what they really want is impossible.

My client Jordan continued to hit his upper limits throughout our initial year of coaching. As a successful financial advisor, he set his sights on being first in his office, then city, then district, and finally his company. Each time he would hit a new high, he would celebrate and acknowledge his success. But it wasn't long before his self-limiting beliefs reared their ugly selves.

Most recently, he began courting a "whale," a client with assets in excess of $80 million dollars, which for any financial advisor can be a year-making win. Our session began with the news he was working with this gentleman to take on the majority of his assets, and his excitement about the prospect of winning his largest client to date. Soon the excitement gave way to doubt and apprehension. As is normal in my clients' sessions, we began to dissect and disassemble each perceived block.

"What if he wants to speak to a client of mine with as many assets as he has?"

"I'm awesome. But am I?"

"I want to but I'm not sure if I can because ..."

By the end of our session, like so many others I've had, Jordan said, *"So basically all of my reasons for not going for it are complete nonsense and I should just go for it?"* Yes. Yes to Jordan and to you.

The truth is that what determines your success is, in large part, how much you believe you can succeed, so for the purposes of our conversation, let's ask what comes first and is most important in achievement: the achievement of a goal *or* the belief that the goal can be achieved *or* believing you deserve to achieve the goal *or* committing to the goal? *Yes!*

You must think you can achieve your goals and outcomes. You must then believe achieving your goals and outcomes is possible. You must believe you deserve to achieve the goals and outcomes you truly desire. Finally, you must be absolutely, 100% committed to achieving those same goals and outcomes and be willing to do whatever it takes to achieve them.

You have to think you can.

When you don't think you can achieve an outcome, you simply won't achieve that outcome. It is as simple as that. However, when you think you can, you have the beginnings of the achievement of that goal. Thinking you can is the first glimmer of possibility showing itself to you. Seeing that possibility of achievement and thinking that achieving your goal could be true are crucial to your success.

The fun part comes right after a goal has been conceived. When you think about your goal, see yourself achieving it in your mind's eye. When you can do just that simple first step, you have set the possibility wheels in motion.

To Think: *I think about my goal all the time and see it as already achieved.*

To Do: Make it a motion picture in your mind that lasts two to three minutes. Turn your motion picture into a twice-daily visualization exercise.

You have to believe you can.

Thinking is just the first step. *Believing* is another level in the process of goal achievement. How much do you believe in yourself in general? This belief, or lack of belief in yourself, factors in heavily. When you think about something you would like to achieve, whether or not you believe this, too, is something you can achieve will determine the end result then and there.

21

We all come equipped with the ability to believe absolutely in our abilities and ourselves. Unfortunately, we confront multiple people, situations, and events that cause us to doubt our abilities. If upon reading this idea, you find yourself lacking in self-confidence and belief, now is absolutely the time to challenge your lack of belief and begin to build a new level of self-confidence.

To Believe: *I believe I can achieve my goal.*

To Do: Make a list of your accomplishments to date. Put that list where you can see it often (as a Post-It® on your computer monitor, as a list on your bathroom mirror, or on a note pad next to your bed) and be sure to review it twice a day.

You have to believe you deserve what you want.

Now we're gettin' crazy! What do you believe you deserve? What should you believe you deserve? In a word: everything. It is my belief (and I'm the author, so that makes me the expert) that just because you're a human being walking this planet you deserve anything and everything you would like to have. Deserving it doesn't mean you will just have it handed to you without a lot of smart planning, hard work, and effort, but nonetheless, *you deserve whatever you want and would like to achieve.*

You can choose to take on my belief and be off to the races, or you can spend some time figuring out if I'm right. Either way, get to the place where you feel in your heart you deserve your desired outcomes, and that positive mental space in turn will help you to get there faster, easier and while you're enjoying the process.

To Believe: *I believe I deserve everything I desire, including success!*

To Do: Make the mental shift into believing you deserve success by affirming "I deserve success" hundreds or even thousands of times a day until you believe it. Ask your mom, spouse, or best friend what you deserve to achieve. Chances are they will say what I said (and no, we haven't conspired). It's up to you to step up and into total belief in your deservability (your "how much do I feel like I deserve this"). Do it now.

You have to commit and follow through.

I once heard, "99% commitment sucks. 100% commitment *rocks.*" I believe it to be true, it has certainly been true for me. You might be afraid or concerned that you'll fail. You might feel that if you give it your all, you still might come up short. You might want to avoid putting yourself out there, because you're afraid you might get hurt.

When you commit to something, in this case a goal you desire to achieve, with your whole heart, soul, and being, you become unstoppable. It's a simple step, this "being committed thing." But being 100% committed sometimes isn't easy because if you're honest with yourself, there can be a smidge of doubt in the back of your mind. This shred of doubt is what could be holding you back.

So what?

Isn't the point of a big goal to become a better version of you? It is for me! The spoils that come with achieving a goal are just the icing on the giant cupcake. In the process, I find out what I'm made of, learn a lot about myself (and those around me), and raise my personal standards even higher. These same side benefits of commitment will show up for you, too. It's fun when you think about it, isn't it?

I challenge you to stop standing in your own way and commit whole-heartedly to what you truly want. Step out in faith, *faith in yourself,* and when you do, the results will surprise you.

The actions that follow the commitment won't come easily, yet they will come easier than they would have had you kept a little in reserve "just in case." The more committed you are, literally the easier it will be to follow through on the action steps you choose as part of your plan.

To Commit: *I commit 100% to achieving {goal} by {date}.*

To Do: Commit to doing your daily actions *daily.* No matter what. If you're an STMA-er, that means checking the boxes on your Dashboard *every single day.*

Plan A and Plan B?

I'm sure you can guess what happens when you have only Plan A? That's right, sparky! <u>Plan A works out</u>. Part of success is, as I mentioned, committing 100%. What I often see is professionals create a Plan A, *"Coach, this is what I truly want."* Then they create a Plan B, *"But, I'm willing to settle for this."*

No, no, no, no. When there is no Plan B, Plan A tends to work out. I know you know this, and yes, I just said it twice. Having Plan A, and only Plan A, and working that plan like your life depends upon it, is *the* golden key to your success.

I personally believe I'm successful because I didn't have any other options. No dad to call to cover my bills. No close friends I could ask for money. No skill set based on advanced education I could fall back on. For me, it was Plan A and only Plan A. Guess what? Plan A has worked out.

I'm not saying commit to Plan A, and the achievement of your Plan A will be easy peasy. In reality, you will probably be faced with many situations that will challenge your commitment. You may indeed experience setback after denial after obstruction after holdup after delay after obstacle. (Sorry about that.) Chances are your path won't be a straight line; it will include steps back and steps to the side.

I have only ever had a Plan A, but Plan A has been changed, revised, updated, expanded, contracted, altered and reconsidered more times than I can count. When I published *The Successful Single Mom* in 2009, I thought for sure I was on the express train to Oprah. My goal was to get that book into the hands of as many of the 13 million single moms in the United States as quickly as possible, because I just knew it could help them. I also knew Oprah had the platform that could facilitate that … or so I thought.

But after the launch and initial excitement over the book, and what seemed like a wasted $20,000 on an ineffective PR firm, I second-guessed my plans and intentions when book sales fell flat. While I had penciled out additional books in the series, and even followed up with *The Successful Single Mom Cooks! Cookbook,* the books didn't catch on as quickly as I thought they would, so I turned my full attention back to my coaching business.

But between 2009 and 2011, I noticed book sales continued to increase, and each month more books were sold than the month before. Then I released the ebook versions, and put them for sale everywhere ebooks are sold and that's when the magic started to happen.

If I had pulled the plug on the project completely, I would have missed out on what's happening present day. I'm certifying facilitators to deliver the *Single Mom Transformation Program* I used with single moms to write the book. I've completed another several books in the series. Because I have published a successful series, another amazing opportunity opened up for me. I thought I knew what was possible and what wasn't possible, but it's a really cool fact that my current reality is even better than my previous imagination could cook up.

See what I mean about revising, rethinking and updating your Plan A? You don't even know the goodness in store for you when you craft and commit to your Plan A.

Once you've settled on your Plan A, the plan that must work out, there's an important psychological shift and commitment you will need to make. In your mind, you must become "the ant that moved the plant." Ants are a terrific analogy for the route to success. They will go over, under, around, or through whatever gets in their way. They never stop moving, and neither should you. Take the word impossible and turn it into "I'm Possible."

You *can* achieve your goals, you *should* achieve your goals, and you *deserve* to achieve your goals. Period.

In the end, it takes a tremendous amount of courage to go for what you truly want out of your life, your career, and your relationships. Tap into the courage that lies within you and let today be the first day of your amazing journey to success. What is possible for you is whatever you can believe is possible for you. Sometimes it's even better!

Know that and keep reading. We're making a new reality, people.

"Action that is not intentional, then combined with a belief in the desired outcome, is wasted action." ~Honorée Corder

<u>Chapter Three:</u>
Your Vision Becomes Your Reality

"Fear not that you will dream too big and miss.
Focus and act so that you aim high and hit!"
~Honorée Corder

This book is about making your vision your reality. For that to happen, there are steps you can take to set the wheels in motion right away, and steps you can take almost to ensure your vision does indeed become your reality.

We've spent some time laying the groundwork, and I have shared some of the steps you can take that will begin to move you in the direction of your vision, goals, and dreams. Make no mistake, your STMA isn't just about what happens over 100 days. It is about what you want to happen and what is going to happen for the rest of your life. Personally and professionally, you are going to notice a shift in your direction based upon what you learn and do over the course of your first 100 days.

If this were "the rest of your life Program," you would not have the same level of urgency because psychologically "the rest of your life" feels like a really long time and could mean you have a really long time to get things done. I am working under the assumption that you, like me, want your vision to become your reality sooner rather than later. Do I even need to mention there is no telling how much time we actually have anyway? I didn't think so.

29

If you and I are on the same page, and what you want is to become more effective and efficient so you can reach your goals sooner, let's dive in to creating a vision that will literally change the course of your life. Before you can begin your Day 1, you absolutely must have a compelling long-term vision, and one heck of a fierce 100-day vision.

Are you ready? Let's begin!

Your Vision

Vision is what you see in your mind's eye, not something you see externally. You don't leave on vacation without knowing your destination, and this journey into the next 100 days is no different. The first step in creating a solid 100-day Plan is the creation of your 100-day vision.

If you've never created a true vision before, it may seem like an exercise that is vague and intangible. The long-term benefits, in this case, your next 100 days, are absolutely beneficial and substantial and help you create the results that can be simply amazing. Your vision, once crystalized, will literally pull you forward. It will get you up early and keep you up late. It will keep you excited, even when you do experience those inevitable challenges, you get off-track, sick, or your progress is slower than you'd like. Indeed, your vision is the glue that holds this whole train together.

Your vision is your "what." When you close your eyes and think of what you truly want, you'll find that a picture of those desires appears on the mental screen of your mind. Even before you can formulate your 100-day vision, I encourage you to envision something much longer-term, such as five or ten years. What's the longer term vision you're working toward? Is it the sale of your business, hiring an assistant, creating a few leveraged streams of income, bringing an associate on board to lighten your load, hiring an entire team to run your business, the acquisition of other businesses, or to join the $250K Club? There's no right or wrong answer, the answer is your best and honest answer. Write down five things you want to have accomplished if you were five or ten years in the future. Here are some ideas to get you started:

- Own a business that produces $5M/year in gross income
- Have completed my first Ironman triathlon (marathon, 10K, etc.)
- Be married
- Own my own home outright
- Payoff my car, debt, home, student loans, etc.
- Create a leveraged stream of income in excess of $10,000/month
- Hire a full-time or part-time assistant that stays with me for 10 years

If you're having trouble getting started, you may not be convinced of the power of creating a vision. All right, I'll take that as a challenge and do my best to convert you to a bona-fide enthusiastic vision-creator. Here are just a few reasons why visioning is something you should do:

- Visioning breaks you out of boundary thinking. As you open your mind and your mind's eye to new possibilities, you will begin to shed previous limitations.

- Visioning provides continuity and avoids the stutter effect of planning fits and starts. Having a defined, clear vision that is reviewed and visualized often – i.e., multiple times daily – will help you avoid the "New Year's Eve Syndrome" ... where goals are set and then forgotten in about two weeks (until the next New Year or you start another 100 days)!

- Your vision automatically identifies your future direction and purpose. It grabs hold of your interest, strengthens your commitment, and promotes laser-like focus. When there is a clear picture in your mind of where you're going, it is always there, accessible and readily available to pull you in the right direction.

- Visioning encourages openness to unique and creative solutions. As you hold your clearly defined vision, the ways to make that vision happen become clear. Your subconscious mind works on your behalf to spot potential opportunities, prospects, and possibilities you might otherwise have missed.

- Visioning promotes and builds confidence. Have you ever noticed how a person who has a purpose and a vision carries himself or herself in a certain way? They are positive, upbeat, and yes, confident. Your confidence is magnetic, attracting to you your clearly defined vision, and that very same vision can work magic for you.

Are you convinced? You have already created in your life what you have previously held as a vision, even if you didn't realize that's what you were doing. The life you live now is the result of what was probably not a carefully crafted vision. Now is the time to use your subconscious mind through the use of this picturing tool to create what you truly desire, this time on purpose and with purpose. Think of vision as clear imagination, only this time you're using directed imagination and creating your future one magical moment at a time.

Your Visioning Exercise

Start the process of creating your vision by daydreaming. Begin to imagine and create a colorful, clear picture in your mind what your business and life will look like when time, energy, people, space, and money are no object. What areas of your business need a clearer vision? How can your marketing, business development, products, services, or even customer service be markedly improved? What areas of your life aren't working as well as you would like? Are you in an empowering relationship that is mutually beneficial? Are you as strong, fit, financially sound, balanced, and fulfilled as you wish to be?

Create an overall vision for this next 100 days based upon your longer-term vision and then break your vision down into focus areas, such as desired revenue and income, the size of your company, and where and how you want to live. Then create a unique vision for each of those areas. If you haven't already created your vision, begin by starting five to ten years in the future. Describe in vivid detail what your ideal day looks like. Include a description of your surroundings (office, employees, clients, family, and friends). Now work backward to your Day 1 from that vision. Describe what that vision looks like on Day 100, day 75, day 50, and then day 25. Ask yourself, "What is my preferred future?" being sure to

- Draw on your beliefs, mission, and mental picture of your model environment.
- Describe in detail what you want to see in the future.
- Be specific to each area of your life.
- Be positive and inspired.
- Be open to a massive upgrade, lots of changes, and a really big leap!

Here are some questions to get you started creating your vision:

- In your preferred future, what time does your day start? End? How many hours do you put in at the office, and how is your day structured?
- Who is with you? Your success is determined in large part by the people you surround yourself with, and it is time to become clear about whom you want to attract into your life in the future. We'll address this more in *Chapter 7, "Who's on Your Bench?"*
- What activities do you want included in your days, weeks, months, and years?
- What types of clients and customers do you have? Create an ideal client list with at least 25 characteristics of the model client.

Include everything from age, income, and attitude to how they receive information and services from you and how often they refer new business to you.

- Where is your office located? Do you have multiple locations? Do you work from home, in the office, or from both places? Be sure to include the type of equipment you work with, all those neat furnishings, plants, pictures, etc.
- Do you have business partners, sales people, investors, employees? How many?
- What is your ideal living space? Where is it located? What do you drive?
- Where do you vacation? With whom? How often?
- Define your friends and other significant relationships.

Other thought-provoking and helpful questions:

- What will you gain from achieving your vision?
- What will the world gain from you achieving your vision?
- Who is going to help you?
- Who is going to help you enjoy the rewards?
- Where will you work on your vision?
- Where will you celebrate its achievement?
- When do you want to achieve different aspects of your vision?
- When are you going to start working on your vision?

- Why on earth are you going to dedicate your time, talents, and resources to work toward this vision?
- Why must you achieve your vision?
- Why are you worth your vision?

Brainstorm. Be specific. Be playful. Be creative. Make the vision of your life the way you want it. After all, it's your life, your business, your vision.

Coach's NOTE: It is important to put your vision in writing. There is power in the written word. Just the act of writing down what you want sets the creative process in motion. Give yourself enough uninterrupted, focused time to go from start to finish of your first draft. I recommend blocking two to three hours to complete the questions above. Then, let your vision sit for a while and come back to it after you've had time to reflect upon it. Your vision is alive; it is living and constantly-evolving. Keep in mind that what you think you want may actually not be what comes to fruition, but what comes to fruition may actually be way better!

Vision Killers

As you engage in the visioning process, you may encounter obstacles that also happen to be people. Just because you are on board with your new destiny doesn't mean everyone around you will or even can be. Be alert to the fact that you may encounter the following vision killers and be ready to ignore them.

> **Tradition:** Be careful of the phrase "But we've always done it this way."

Fear of ridicule: Most often the people who criticize are those who have neglected to create their own vision and who come from a place of fear instead of power. Have compassion for them but don't listen to them.

Stereotypes of people, conditions, roles, and outcomes: You may hear, "Why do you think you can achieve this?" Your answer: "Why not me?"

Naysayers: Very simply, refuse to listen to anyone who doesn't absolutely 100% support your vision. Period.

Look, some of these folks are wanting to help you, warn you against doing something that could cause you to get hurt, or "lose everything." Most likely, they are coming from a good place and don't mean to inflict the harm that comes from sowing seeds of "you can't succeed." It's just that their advice and intention is run through their own filters, and those filters are often chock-full of limiting beliefs, past failures, and even frustration with their own lack of success.

Should you need some words of encouragement, I believe these from Will Smith in the movie *Pursuit of Happyness,* will do the trick:

> *"Don't ever let somebody tell you 'you can't do something' ... not even me, alright? You got a dream? You got to protect it. People who can't do it themselves, they wanna tell you – "You can't do it!" If you want something, go get it. Period."*

Remember: there is no right or wrong way to write a vision! You should describe in full detail exactly what you desire. It may take up to 20 pages or more, or it may be as simple as one page using bullet points.

Your Purpose: The *Why* Behind the *What*

Knowing what you want is one thing; knowing why you want it is something entirely different. Your vision is what you want; your purpose for getting it is why you want it in the first place. If you just want something for the sake of wanting it, you probably won't ever get it. Over time, the desire for your outcomes will lessen, or the daily distractions of life will quickly take you off track. If, on the other hand, you know exactly why you want what you want, then you have increased your chances of achievement. By how much? I honestly don't know, but I do know this: *it is a lot.*

Let's say your Goal #1 is "$100,000 in new revenue." That's terrific. If a goal is set correctly, it is specific, measurable, attainable, risky, and time-sensitive {SMART} goal. We will discuss goal-setting in-depth in the next chapter. For now, we're making the assumption your goal meets the "acceptable goal-setting criteria." What I don't know, as your coach, is *why* you want to make $100,000. Of course, it is critical you know and feel, i.e., have a strong emotional connection, to your why, too!

Is the goal what your boss or business partner wants? Or is it a little more personal: you want to pay off some debt, buy a new car, move into a new home, or sock some money away for junior's college fund? Do you have a strong, burning desire to achieve your goal, or are you just filling in the blanks and checking the boxes? In other words, what is the purpose – the *why* – behind this goal. What will achieving this vision, and this goal, really give you besides a sense of accomplishment?

Look at it this way: your vision is firewood, your purpose is the gas you pour on the wood before you light the fire. The fire burns brighter, hotter, and longer with lots of gas and just the right match to light it up. Your vision will have the fuel it needs to burn brighter, hotter, and longer when you have a crystal clear purpose.

When you are navigating the stages of the 100 days, you will need a strong, clear vision to keep you going as you encounter those inevitable challenges. Even if you have smooth sailing, and nothing that causes you concern, I promise the enthusiasm with which you set your goals will wane, and at some point you will lose your urgency. What will keep you going, in addition to the structure and accountability of the STMA, will be your internal desire to achieve your vision and the goals that will make that vision a reality.

Case Study

Michelle Daniels is an estate planning attorney client. During our initial work together, she was a partner, in name only at a two-partner firm for almost five years. She brought in more than 70% of the new clients to the firm and handled almost 60% of the work.

Her partner, Herb, brought her in as an associate, and when the time was right, put her name on the door and on the stationery. But he did not change their agreement and continued to pay her a paltry salary, much less than what should have been her compensation. He benefitted from additional partner perks, such as an expense account and a car allowance. He even paid his spouse a salary. Michelle was offered none of these benefits. Through coaching, she eventually got up her courage and asked if Herb would be willing to extend some, if not all, of these same benefits to her. Her first Goal #1, her "what," was to determine if she could stay at her current firm and increase her compensation to an amount we defined. Her "why" was because she and her husband were having a hard time making ends meet, and a reasonable bump in compensation would make their financial situation easier.

We put together a plan to approach Herb after the first 50 days of her 100 days, and in those first 50 days, Michelle upped her efforts to bring in new clients, bill more strategically, and take on more of a leadership role within her firm. However, when she set her meeting with her partner, Herb was unwilling to extend any additional compensation or benefits to her and said he had no plans to for the foreseeable future. So, the answer to her question, "Can I stay at my current firm?" was *no.*

Michelle was incredibly apprehensive about going out on her own and had tough questions about what starting her own firm would entail:

- How will I find new business?
- What if I can't take any of my old clients with me?

- What if my former partner tries to sue me?

There were, of course, many other questions.

Michelle needed a new "what" (her vision) and a new "why" (her purpose).

We calculated what she needed to realize each month in order to not just survive, but thrive as a solo practitioner. Her budget determined the minimum number of hours she needed to bill and the minimum amount of billed dollars she needed to collect. It turned out she needed only to bill and collect just over 18 hours of work each week, which meant a typical workweek of 40-45 hours, divided into her Core Four of doing her work product, rainmaking and business development, keeping current clients happy, and administration, all of which would provide her more than what she needed to thrive in her new practice.

Remember those inevitable challenges I mentioned earlier? Michelle was not immune from them! The same month she found out she was pregnant was the month she started her own firm, which added a new question:

- What if my pregnancy prohibits me from working for a period of time?

Her new Goal #1 was to earn the amount defined in her first 100 days, only this time, there was no salary involved. Her purpose for achieving Goal #1 was to be able to support her family with money to spare and to be able to take time off when the baby arrived without a high stress level. Because she was clear about what she wanted and why she wanted it, the goals we defined were clear, powerful, and achievable with the right plan she had created.

She found an office to rent from another small law firm that had extra space. The firm allowed her to use their equipment, conference room, and even receptionist for a modest monthly fee. Michelle systematically contacted her clients and let them know of her move, and many of them followed her. She set up her systems for generating new business and began networking, utilizing the 12x12 System™, which you will learn about shortly.

Lest you think becoming pregnant was her only challenge, think again! She also had a few other issues to deal with: she had morning sickness for the first several months, she already had a two-year-old daughter, and her husband was laid-off from his teaching job. All during her 100 days, after she had started her own firm.

She committed, and recommitted daily, to her plan and worked it as intentionally and purposefully as she could. The results astounded her: after overhead and expenses, she was able to double her salary within her first 100 days in business. By the time she took a few weeks off to have her baby, she had hired an associate and shared in the expense of an assistant. She reached her Goal #1, met her income requirements, and realized her vision of having a successful practice.

Michelle represents the goals and challenges of many of my clients: the bigger the game that's played, the bigger the challenges tend to be. That's why a strong plan combined with an even stronger commitment is a must.

Coach's Challenge: Your Vision and Purpose

If you haven't already, now is the time to work on your long-term vision, your 100-day vision, and purpose. Stop here, right now, and create your vision. Do your "big vision" (the long-term 5 or 10-year version) first and, then craft your 100-day vision. You'll turn it into a brief 3-4 sentence paragraph and add it to your initial 100-Day Plan. Before you can create any goal, a clear picture of your overall vision must be present in your mind's eye.

If now isn't the time, then pull out your calendar and schedule time for two things: 1) at least a two-hour block to complete your visions (long-term and 100-day) and purpose and 2) another two-hour block to read the next chapter and set your 100-day goals.

*"In order for any system or strategy to work,
it is up to you to take the first step. The structure
will set you free!"* ~Honorée Corder

Chapter Four:
BHAGs: Big, Hairy, Audacious Goals Get You Up Early & Keep You Up Late

"Committed eats impossible for breakfast."
~Honorée Corder

Identify your most important goals, and suddenly you're well on your way to figuring out how to make them happen. As if by magic, you can and will develop the attitudes, abilities, skills, resources, connections, and financial capacity to reach them. You will begin seeing previously overlooked opportunities and possibilities. There seems to be a way through to a successful outcome that before you got really clear, there really didn't seem a way.

You must:

- Know what you want,
- Believe it's possible for you, and
- Shake your money-maker (get moving).

If your vision and purpose got you excited, crafting clearly defined goals is going to set you on fire (or at least light your fire). Having a crystal-clear vision and purpose, as you may have discovered, makes you want to get into action, get moving, and get things done. Let's help you to set some goals that will intentionally steer your positive and outcome-producing energy in the right direction.

Either You're SMART, or You're Not

SMART stands for *specific, measureable, attainable, risky, and time-sensitive*. SMART goals are the bomb-diggity. They eliminate all doubt, inaction, and lack (of time, money, space, people you really like, clients, and so much more). You may have heard this acronym before, and it begs the question: have you really put it to use with regards to your goals? If you haven't, and you probably haven't, chances are you have lots of goals that are actually just hopes, dreams, thoughts, and wishes. You don't want to set just any old goals for your STMA. No, sir, these goals are special because you are on a mission now; you have a vision and a purpose.

And now that you have that vision and purpose, it is time to set some awesome goals based on that white-hot vision you've crafted. Don't waste another minute before you make sure your goals meet the following criteria:

Specific

A specific goal gets achieved. A wishy-washy, "I'm not sure what I want goal" won't be. It's as simple as that. Refer to your vision and purpose when setting your goals, all along the way asking yourself some powerful questions. Try these:

- Based on my long-term vision, what do I want to accomplish *the absolute most* over the next 100 days?
- What are the two most important professional areas I must laser-focus on,

such as marketing, business development, client development, or customer service?

- What is one area, personally, I must make measurable improvement in, such as making myself smokin' hot, or getting my emotions in check, or living on the spiritual plane, or paying off debt or a vehicle, or even making my marriage magical?

- If these 100 days are going to be a bona-fide success, what do I need to accomplish and how great am I going to feel about it when I do?

If you have a goal of "amassing a fortune and achieving global domination," you won't be able to complete all of it in the next 100 days, but you can put aside a defined dollar amount or percentage of your income. You can write a few chapters in a book, buy some art for your office, schedule and pay for your next vacation, or set the dates for the next year of marketing events. Rest assured you can make progress, and you can get into very strong momentum during the next 100-days.

Measurable

What gets measured and re-measured gets attention. Everything else does not. Therefore, you absolutely must establish concrete criteria for measuring progress, initially and continually, toward the attainment of each and every goal you set.

When you measure your progress, you stay on track, reach or exceed your targeted goals, and experience the exhilaration of achievement that spurs you on to continued effort required to reach your goal. And when you don't, you don't. Stay

47

tuned, for we're going to dive more deeply into daily tracking in the next chapter.

To determine if your goal is measurable, ask questions, such as

- How much? As in: how much money? How much time?
- How many? As in: how many new clients? How many miles or reps?
- How will I or anyone else know when the goal has been accomplished?

We have a mechanism for continual measurement: your Dashboard. You'll learn more about it shortly, and over at least the next 100-days, you will spend a lot of time with your Dashboard.

Attainable

I play pretty fast and loose on "attainable" because my belief is there's always a way if you're committed, but you have to have a plan, and you have to work that plan like you're all out of bubble gum and you really, really want more bubble gum more than you want life itself. If you're wavering on this issue, refer to Chapter 2.

There are some exceptions: You're a woman, and you want to play for the New Orleans Saints. *No sale.* Best we could get you is ownership. (Now that's a great goal!)

Goals that seemed almost impossible move closer and become attainable, not because your goals shrink, but because you grow and expand to match them. When you list your goals you build your self-image. You see yourself as worthy of these goals, and you develop the traits and personality that allow you to possess them.

That's why getting clear on what you want and why you're worthy and deserving really help accelerate this process.

Risky

WAIT! What do you mean, *"risky,"* coach?

Risky means the goal, literally, makes you a bit nauseous. You know this goal is something you really want to achieve, you know it's something that's achievable, and you know it's something achievable by YOU if you put your all into it. However, it will be a risk for you to name it and then do your best to claim it. It's always worth attempting to go after our heart's desires because goals like these tend to make us into the best versions of ourselves. How do you know if you've got the right goals? Thanks for asking, I'm happy to provide the answer:

- If, after you set your goals, you think, "No problem, I've got this," the goal isn't big enough. Try again.
- If, after you set your goals, you think, "There's no way. I'm going to go watch some television," the goal is too big. Try again.
- If, after you set your goals, you think, "I'm going to have to give it everything I've got, but I'm pretty darn sure I can knock this one out of the park with solid, consistent effort, unwavering faith and a smidge of luck,"

then *you've got it!* You've identified the right-sized goal just for you.

Take the risk, go out on the limb, and lean so far out over the ledge you think you might fall off. The risk is worth the effort!

Time

We've got the "time" part covered; you have until your Day 100 to achieve your goals, so I've added another "T" to the process:

Tangible

A goal is tangible when you can experience it with one of the senses: taste, touch, smell, sight, or hearing. When your goal is tangible, or when you tie a tangible goal to an intangible goal, you have a better chance of making it specific and measurable and thus attainable.

Intangible goals are your goals for the internal changes required to reach more tangible goals. They are the personality characteristics and the behavior patterns you must develop to pave the way to success in your career or for reaching some other long-term goal. Because intangible goals are vital for improving your effectiveness, give close attention to tangible ways for measuring them.

Regular Goal to BHAG!

Now that you know the elements of well-set goals, let's get you setting some great goals while almost at the same time creating an amazing plan for their achievement.

Goal-setting time: Put pen to paper or fingers to keyboard and write those *big, hairy audacious goals*

(BHAGs) that make you sit straight up in your chair and get all of your cylinders firing.

A goal I usually see is "Get in shape." A specific and inspiring BHAG would say, "Get in the best shape of my life: I weigh 180 lbs. and have 13% body fat." "I want to increase my billable hours" would be replaced with "I want to double my billing. I bill in excess of $20,000 per month in fees, for a total of $65,000 in 100 days."

Goal-Setting Exercise

1. Pretend today is your birthday. For at least 20 minutes, brainstorm a list of everything you want to achieve over the next 100 days.
2. Review your list and circle the top 3: circle two related to business and one related to you personally.
3. Write down the kind of person it will take to achieve all that you want. Describe character traits, values, beliefs, virtues, and so forth that this person (you!) would embody. List these characteristics under your Empowering Descriptors.

Committed or Just Excited?

Goals don't exist just for the sake of achieving something. Goals help us to become all we're meant to be. They help us find out what we're made of and discover our true capabilities. The fastest path to an achieved goal is the path you're committed to taking.

Let's complete the circle of goal setting. I want you to do one more exercise.

- Write a paragraph about why you're committed to achieving each goal you have set.

Not just why you want to achieve it, but why you're <u>committed</u> to achieving it. Life in general can be hard, even harsh at times. When you feel like you're working your butt off and making no progress whatsoever, these paragraphs about your commitment will be what you refer to. They will stand as mile-markers on your goal highway, enabling you to overcome any resistance you have to continuing forward and see again and again *why* you want your *what*.

Remember this: the chicken is interested, the pig is committed. In this scenario, you are the pig. The pig sacrifices everything to become your dinner, the chicken just provides a little something on the side. If you really must achieve your goals, then you really must be absolutely 100% committed. You are absolutely committed to making your goals come true, right? I know you are!

You've done a lot of work – congratulations! You're laying the foundation for a strong and successful STMA 100-day Program. But it's just beginning to get good, and you haven't even started yet. Much like writing a book or having a baby, creating just the beginning. It's what happens when you've got the book or the baby that's the very best part.

> *"Making a plan is just the first step. The best is yet to come!"* ~Honorée Corder

Chapter Five:
The Power of Laser Focus

"Failure to focus dilutes results. Paying full attention boosts your brain power, strengthens your synaptic connections, and creates the neural pathways that eventually turn your actions into your actuality." ~Honorée Corder

The most powerful aspects of the STMA have to do with the built-in accountability and the structure behind that accountability. Part of the goal of the STMA is to keep you laser focused on your vision and goals for the duration of the 100 days so that your Vision truly does become your Reality.

Coach's Note: You can absolutely use the structure and tools and guide yourself through a successful 100 days. I'm going to suggest that engaging in a more formal type of accountability will exponentially increase your results. More on that coming right up.

You, too, will be amazed when you realize all you can accomplish when you put your mind, energy, and all of your effort into achieving what you set out to achieve.

In the words of one of my clients, *"It's amazing what I can get done when I focus."*

You may or may not know that a laser, by focusing all of its energy in one spot, can literally break through boulders. I want you to see the correlation between a laser's focus and the power of focus you can harness by including it into your daily activities. You have to have the right elements, and you must put your focus and energy on the end result and stay focused on the end result, regardless of what happens around you.

Actions Become Habits

During the pre-work phase of the STMA, using the pre-determined Daily Actions, you will identify your specific Daily Actions. Such as, your morning routine could be the SAVERS practice from *The Miracle Morning*. Your Rainmaking daily action could be to make ten calls to potential prospects, or attend at least one networking meeting. The idea is that eventually the Daily Actions will become your habits. In other words, instead of an action being something you *do*, it actually becomes part of who you *are.*

Let me explain. The regular actions you take eventually become your habits, whether you intend them to or not, and whether they positively contribute to your success or not. At one time, your mother introduced "brushing your teeth" into your life. At first, she took you to the sink and helped you brush your teeth. She taught you how to brush, how long to brush, how to put toothpaste on the toothbrush and how to rinse properly. Eventually, you brushed your teeth with her reminding you morning and night. "Son, did you brush your teeth?" Eventually, you took it upon yourself to brush your teeth and then go show your shiny clean chompers to your mom. Finally, you just brushed your teeth as a matter of habit, sometimes doing it unconsciously as you thought about something else entirely. Brushing your teeth was no longer an action you had to do, it became a part of who you are. Your STMA action items are meant to become your habits – they become just as much a part of who you are and what you do as brushing your teeth.

Some of the habits we have "just happen." We fall into habits that don't serve us, like the afternoon snack from the vending machine, checking email first instead of doing revenue generating activities, watching television instead of reading, or having dessert with every meal.

How cool would it be to automatically do what's necessary to become successful because you have installed the habits that make that happen?

It's imperative that you intentionally identify the actions you want to become your habits, instead of just letting habits show up in your life. The actions you identify as beneficial to achieving your goals will eventually become your habits, therefore choosing them in advance is a critical step in your success.

As part of the STMA, we've identified the Six Daily Actions you need to customize and then act upon on a daily basis in order to achieve your goals, and vision, and to take your *Vision* to *Reality*. Once you've added these actions to your Dashboard, you will use it daily to track how often you actually do those actions. Check all the boxes, and eventually you have a new habit that supports you. Not checking the boxes reveals where you need to implement a new system or strategy to get, and keep, progress toward your goals on track.

Eventually, as the long-term maximum results begin to take effect, your actions will indeed become a habitual part of you. You no longer have to think about doing them; you just do them.

When you first start, you will look at your Dashboard to remind you to do your daily actions. Most likely, you will refer to it as you create your schedule hourly, daily, and weekly. It has been determined there are certain habits that support excellence and success. As luck would have it, you don't have to spend precious time figuring out what you need to do. As I've mentioned, the STMA Program provides the Six Daily Habits you need to consistently execute to get from Point A to Point B as quickly and efficiently as possible. And, without further ado …

The Six Daily Actions are:

- **Your A.M. Routine.** Your A.M. Routine is the part of your day that is just about you. As part of the STMA, you learn how to set yourself up for success on a daily basis. Opportunities come faster when you are mentally, physically, and even spiritually prepared for them. Challenges met with optimism, from a place of strength and power, are handled with ease and grace and overcome more quickly and easily. You will develop a daily practice so you are able to capitalize on opportunities and crush challenges as you continue to make progress toward your goals.

What your daily aptitude for success comes down to is this: you must be mentally and physically prepared to handle the opportunities that come your way. Conversely, you must be prepared to handle the stressors and challenges that pop up. If you don't have any at the moment, rest assured they are coming; however, when you are prepared, you are simply more resourceful. You have heard the phrase, "I'm in such a good mood, and nothing could ruin my day!" You can engineer circumstances, *your circumstances,* to put up a virtual protective field against anything that comes your way. The bonus is you will be able to jump thoughtfully, energetically, and enthusiastically on the opportunities that present themselves as well.

I again suggest you read *The Miracle Morning* by my friend Hal Elrod. He's cracked the code on morning routines, and before you know it, your miracle mornings will produce miracle *results.*

- **Rainmaking.** Rainmaking, also known as business development, is key to anyone's business or practice, and yours is no exception. A constant stream of business must flow through the door in order to exceed last quarter's results and last year's bonus. Daily focus of a minimum of 4 minutes is all that is required to expand your network of strategic partners and prospective clients. You can do more, but you'll always have at least 4 minutes, and those 4 minutes are critical to your success.

You'll use a tool we're introducing to you shortly, The 12x12 System™, to fully focus your efforts.

- **Work Product.** Getting a signed contract is just the beginning. That's when the real fun begins, and you must provide the promised products and services. Scheduling time to execute on what you have promised is also a crucial component to success. Whether this time is in the form of a full day where you are sequestered to do research and draft a brief, complete an entire financial audit, or deliver products, it must be calendared and kept sacred. Be sure to do this work when you are at your best and feel the sharpest. If your best time of day is first thing, that's when you will tackle the items that are most complex and require the majority of your brainpower. If you get into the zone around 10 a.m., get some of the administrative tasks and phone calls out of the way before you use the blocked time to accomplish this most important task.

- **Keeping Current Clients Happy.** Your clients need to hear from you and not just when you're discussing their current matter, return, or transaction. In order for them to know you truly care, reach out at strategic, carefully selected times to say hello, just because. This alters the relationship from transactional to relational. If any client ever feels they are a number and not a name, they are up for grabs, and they will leave you. It's not a matter of *if;* it's a matter of *when.*

Coach's Action: Pick at least three times per year to contact each of your clients, once by phone, once by mail (say with a holiday card or invite to a party or other event), and once in person (if geographically possible). Call to check in on them personally and professionally. Find out what is new in their world. Ask how their most recent transaction or contact with your firm was for them. Find out what else they need (new clients, an introduction, or even a new plumber!) and do your best to provide it. This isn't the time to tell them they haven't paid their invoice or to tell them all documents were filed on time. This call is more personal in nature because the best client-provider relationships are personal in nature. You actually care about your clients and want them to know that, so show them you care.

- **Administration.** Administrative work is, without question, the majority of my clients' least favorite thing to do. Look at it this way: without sending invoices and logging in your time, invoices won't get sent, and you won't get paid. This is, as they say, "no good." I suggest scheduling administrative time for when you're least effective. For some, that is first thing in the morning. For me, by around 4 p.m., I'm best at answering emails, preparing invoices, and doing follow-up. I don't have to be as sharp to do those activities, so I save them for the end of the day.

- **Personal time with friends and family.** You aren't working so hard *just* because it is fun and fulfilling, although my wish for you is that you find bliss and joy in your work. You are most definitely working hard to enjoy time and fun experiences and to create great memories with the ones you love. Work is about being able to afford doing the things you enjoy doing. Put the most significant people in your life right where they belong – on your calendar! Schedule weekly date nights, one-on-one time with each of your kids, guys and girls nights, golf outings, 3-day weekends, and at least a few weeks of vacation each year. Taking intentional breaks will accomplish several things: you will know when you're going to get a much-needed break to rest, recharge, and re-energize. So will your friends and family. They, too, are working hard to see you succeed.

Each of the above Six Daily Actions needs time on your calendar every single day, and if not every single day, then several times per week *or* a significant amount of blocked time during the week. You may choose to do all of your administrative work on Friday afternoons and work four days straight on work product. That time frame is fine as long as the other daily actions receive focus, too, and get your intentional, on-going, and regular attention as well.

As you focus on these actions and upgrade them to habits, you will think differently because you will act differently. Dare I say *better?* Yes, yes, I do. *Better.*

Habits Become Your Identity

As I said above, habits eventually become not just something you do; they become who you are. You brushed your teeth this morning before you went to work, and you will brush them tonight before bed. You don't think about this habit, you don't procrastinate doing it, and you don't do it some days and not others. Brushing your teeth is not something you do; it's actually part of who you are.

Eventually, the Six Daily Actions become your Six Daily Habits, and then they become part of your natural routine because they have literally become you. There's no question about it, you do them. Identifying the actions and putting them on your Dashboard is the first step in the process.

This process is very similar to the Four Stages of Competence. The original model was around learning. Here we have adapted it for use when integrating new habits as part of the STMA.

The Four Stages of Competence

1. **Unconscious incompetence.** An individual does not understand or know how to do something and does not necessarily recognize the deficit. They may deny the usefulness of the skill. The individual must recognize their own incompetence and the value of the new skill before moving on to the next stage. The length of time an individual spends

in this stage depends on the strength of the stimulus to learn. In this stage, you may be unaware of the most effective and useful habits you must have as a productive and successful businessperson.

2. **Conscious incompetence.** Though the individual does not understand or know how to do something, he or she does recognize the deficit, as well as the value of a new skill in addressing the deficit. The making of mistakes can be integral to the learning process at this stage. Here you have discovered what you are not doing. Perhaps you don't know how to do these newly-identified tasks and are trying to grasp how to integrate them into your days? This awareness is a catalyst for learning and growth.

3. **Conscious competence.** The individual understands or knows how to do something; however, demonstrating the skill or knowledge requires concentration. It may be broken down into steps, and there is heavy conscious involvement in executing the new skill. Now you have identified your daily actions and are using your Dashboard to remind you what needs to be done and to help keep track of these identified best-action steps.

4. **Unconscious competence.** The individual has had so much practice with a skill that it has become "second nature" and can be performed easily. As

a result, the skill can be performed while executing another task. The individual may be able to teach it to others, depending upon how and when it was learned.

By the end of your first 100 days, you have begun the process of building your "habit-forming muscles," and to solidify the habits that will last a lifetime all while ensuring your success.

The STMA is instrumental in not just identifying which habits are the most useful to acquire. It takes you through the stages automatically as part of the process to unconscious competence, or as I like to say, "your habit becomes part of who you are." Some people workout a few times a week until they lose weight and gain strength or until they complete a program. Other people workout because exercise is an integral part of their lifestyle. What we're going for here is *lifestyle* as it pertains to your business growth and success.

Focus

Once your Six Daily Actions are identified, your daily focus on, and execution of, them is instrumental in your success. Your focus, once easily broken, becomes more important. As you begin to make progress and strengthen your results-building muscles, your actions become the habits that drive your behavior. Habits are relied upon unconsciously, and they carry you from day to day without you having to think about them.

What breaks your focus? Many things, of course, can and will cause you to break contact with your progress. Any one of the following can break your focus:

- Illness {yours, your spouse's, children, or other family members}
- Legal matters
- Vacations
- Holidays
- Natural events
- National or world economic events

What happens when your focus is broken? Possible loss of momentum, for a moment, a short time, or, tragically, forever. The STMA and the points of accountability are in place to make sure that when you lose focus, even for a second, you are able to regain it without losing the momentum you've gained.

The stages of the STMA are brought to your attention for a reason, as you will go through each of them as the program progresses. You will be excited during the first days and weeks. You will feel complacent or lose your feelings of urgency at some point. You will experience a challenge or two that will challenge your commitment to the Program.

The trick is to know they are coming and prepare for them in advance. You will have challenges you don't know are coming, and you'll weather those more easily, too. When you have challenges is the time the systems you have in place (or identify the ones you need to put in place) will make all of the difference, as will the habits you are carefully installing into your programming.

Systems Save the Day (Week, Month, and Year)

There are so many things to do and seemingly with so little time. The only way you can be productive and get things done is to be efficient and effective. That means having systems in place to guide exactly how and even when you do your Six Daily Actions and, frankly, everything else. What we're doing here is adding a level of intention to every action you take every day, which will drastically cut down the amount of time you need to complete each item on your to do list.

Here are the key strategies for systematizing just about everything:

Identify how to do your most valuable activities. Make a list of what you need to do to complete each activity efficiently. Because "Rainmaking" is a key Daily Action, it goes on the calendar every day or at least for a measurable time each week. To put a system in place, you will want to make a list of what you need to have in front of you to complete the action of "Rainmaking" efficiently. For example, I have my 12x12 accessible for immediate use (mine "lives" on my Desktop), along with my calendar, and I block off time to send emails and make phone calls. I take it a step further and calendar what I call "Blocked Time" not only to complete my daily Rainmaking activities, but also to calendar time to *do* the rainmaking. In other words, I already know before I reach out to someone when I have time set aside to meet with them, make an introduction, or do the pitch. Some days I truly only focus on Rainmaking just four minutes; other days it is an hour or two. Always

65

blocked time, always focused, always intentional, always efficient.

You will want a system for each activity you need to complete, for having systems in place saves time, money, and energy. You can indeed get more done in less time when you know exactly what you need at your disposal to complete the task. This approach is similar to watching someone cook on television. They already have the ingredients they need, in the right amounts, in front of them. They just combine the ingredients and voila – very soon dinner is served! Attempting to complete a task without everything you need on hand can double, triple or exponentially multiply the amount of time it takes to complete a task. This is unnecessary wasted time and action, so if you have been in the habit of being woefully unprepared in the past, stop making life, business, and success harder on yourself by making being prepared part of your identity.

Identify the system you need. You ask your assistant to do something for you, and they happily return to your office several hours or days later, completed project in hand. You then realize it wasn't done the way you wanted it, and worse, it will have to be done again from scratch. What happened? Most likely, you did not communicate effectively exactly what and how you wanted the project completed. You may have missed steps or details that were critical for said project to be done just the way you wanted.

Make a list of key activities and create a "how to" guide for yourself and others so each action can be done in a timely fashion exactly the way you want it. We don't want missing steps or details in your system, so you need a system for creating your system. This system starts with questions. You are going to drill down each of your Six Daily Actions into the steps, actions, micro-actions, and details needed to complete the task as quickly, easily, and efficiently as possible.

Ask yourself these questions:

- What do I need or want to do?
- How long do I need to do it?
- What do I need at my fingertips or in place to complete the task efficiently?
- Do I need to be in a certain place or location? If so, where?
- Is anyone else needed to complete the project? If so, what does he/she need to know to be efficient and effective or at least present?
- Can the project be completed in one sitting or do I need to calendar multiple blocks of time?

Once you've completed each system, take some time away from what you've done, and then go back and review to discover what possibly might be missing.

Remember to develop a system for getting back on track after a break, illness, or challenge. I'll share what I do, and what I suggest you do:

- Calendar appointments for the afternoon of the first day back at work. Your cure for the "holiday break" hangover is to get right back into the deep end of the pool. Don't

67

hang out in the shallow end of the pool, which to me means you'll start calendaring things after you get back. Starting right after you return, reach out to important contacts prior to the break and calendar meetings, lunches, and events.

- If coming back from a personal not-so-serious illness, give yourself a bit of extra time to get caught up with emails, phone calls, and work product, or give yourself an extra hour or two for those activities and then dive right back into your normal schedule. It's like ripping off a Band-Aid: just do it and the pain will subside more quickly. However! If you are recovering from serious illness, injury or surgery, I suggest blocks of time to work that are shorter and less intense at first. Unnecessary stress and lack of rest will cause a slower recovery time. I'm sure work is not more important than your health, and giving yourself the time you need to get back up to full speed may make the difference between getting back into the zone faster and causing a relapse.

- Get mentally ready to dive back in rather than easing back in, after a break. Rest fully. Don't check emails, texts, or phone messages. It doesn't matter if you're in Spain on a two-week vacation or in bed with the flu; be on a break, and a break means you're not a businessperson, you're just a person who is resting, rejuvenating, recharging, and healing. The side dish benefit is once you return to your desk, you'll be really ready to dive in and tackle what's waiting for you!

It will probably occur to you to develop systems for activities not mentioned here, activities that have nothing do with a successful STMA. That's great – systems set you free and save the day, so the more the merrier. I have systems for working out, fixing healthy meals for my family, planning and going on vacation, and cleaning the house. I have systems for each of my Six Daily Actions, writing books, and completing other important projects. If I didn't, I would remain frozen and overwhelmed by the unending to do list I've penciled out. If you're frozen with regards to getting something done, develop a system. Then take one step, then another, and then another. Soon, you will have completed the project, even in the midst of what can only be characterized as the insanity of every day life, and be darn glad you did.

The more systems you have in place, the more efficient and effective you will be. The bonus is you will have a lower stress level, and you will accomplish what is truly important to you. Even better, this level of focus and attention will eventually become habitual and will drive how you do everything. Trust me when I say a low-stress, high-productive business and life are very cool places to hang out. I look forward to seeing you there!

"Coaching is a series of conversations, encouragements, and ideas that lead to the creation of your destiny." ~Honorée Corder

Chapter Six:
What's Your I AM?

"The two most powerful words put together are: "I am." Be ruthlessly discriminating about what words you choose to use with them." ~Honorée Corder

I AM. Two of the most powerful words in the English language (or any language), for what you put after them shapes your reality.

I am awesome! I am fabulous! I am terrific! I am beautiful! I am capable!

Do these statements resemble what you say when you talk to yourself? Or do these sound more like you:

I am tired. I am bad at {insert something here}. I am incapable. I am unable. I am a failure.

If you are saying things after the "I AM" that are disempowering to you, it's time for an upgrade. I have heard people say, "I am not able to do that, I am always late, I am always out of time," etc. Whoa! Stop the truck and back that sucker up!

The only things you're not able to do are the things you tell yourself you're not able to do. Your self-talk is critical to your success. Either you speak to yourself in an empowering way, or you don't. If you don't, you're doing yourself a major, colossal, avoidable disservice.

I've seen people start their first 100 days enthusiastically, charged up, and ready to go; however, after few successes, missteps, and many challenges, they are ready to give up. When we dig just below the surface to find out what's going on, it's inevitably their self-talk that needs an overhaul. Their "I AMs" are directing them down a path, and it's not the path they want to be on.

If negative self-talk describes you to a "t", I understand. There is a tendency to speak unkindly to ourselves, and it's so prevalent I would consider it the norm in our society. The good news is you can easily correct how you speak to yourself, and it's free! Smile.

As a professional, you are expected to maintain a happy, positive attitude. This ultimate desired state of mind can be difficult to achieve when a challenge comes across your path: there's more month than money, the long to do list keeps you from getting to work on time, or you run out of milk after you've poured the cereal. It's easy to maintain a positive attitude when things are going great, but it's much harder to maintain control of your attitude when they aren't.

In addition, your inner circle consists of the people who actually really care if you're having a good day or a bad day, but there are those who don't care. I recently had a client who was over-sharing with her STMA group. She was telling them about her tax bill, her challenges as a single mom, and how a few clients were holding off on work. I told her, "It's not that they don't care, it's that they don't care." No one outside of your inner circle wants or needs to know when you're going through a tough patch. Save your problems for "your people": your mom, spouse, best friend, coach, or even therapist.

Also be working on your "I AM" statements and your self-confidence, and your attitude so you don't have so many stressors you need to be concerned about.

Remember these words: the real pros consistently perform at their peak, not because they're always in control of their circumstances, but because they're in control of their self-talk and attitude.

Without question, your positive mental attitude starts with your "I AM."

Perhaps you didn't realize that every single time you say "I AM" in a sentence, you are simultaneously sending a direct order and a confirmation to your brain exactly how you truly feel about yourself and what you expect. You are actually sending a command to your subconscious mind and telling every cell of your body how to respond.

If we go even deeper, the spiritual concept of the "I AM" is a prayer declaring exactly what it is you want to have happen.

One of my clients, Alisha, had some real issues with her job and her co-workers. She didn't want to be at her unfulfilling job, and she especially disliked the two-hour commute from just outside of Philadelphia to New York City in which she was carpooling with unfriendly people. I shared with her the benefits of affirmations and using "I AM" statements to shift her focus and energy. She started using them and confirmed she felt better, but still felt stifled in her commuting environment.

We came up with the idea to tell everyone in the car the psychological and physiological attributes of the "I AM" statements on the brain. She started saying her "I AM" statements quietly, and then slowly one by one, the others joined in. Each time they said a new set, they got louder and with more enthusiasm. Finally, they got so loud and excited they ended up in complete laughter. A shift had occurred for her and her carpool mates.

On the way home, Alisha started talking only about the little tiny successes she had that day, and the others started examining their day too, determining it was a pretty good day as well. By keeping the talk positive and focused on only good things, she found that the four hours in the car flew by and she was actually looking forward to her commute, instead of dreading it.

A few weeks later, she told me that not only was her job so much better, but also everyone in her carpool had become close friends. Every morning, they do the "I AM" statements, and every afternoon they talk about their successes. Now they are beginning to understand that they are the ones who create their reality. They never got into talking about spiritual side of saying affirmations, but my client did say a few prayers of thanks for this miracle.

Here is how to get the most out of your "I AM" statements:

On your way to work or on the way to taking your kids to school, have everyone in the car say, out loud and with as much enthusiasm as possible:

- "I AM brilliant"
- "I AM articulate"
- "I AM loved"
- "I AM appreciated"
- "I AM kind"
- "I AM generous"
- "I AM enthusiastic"
- "I AM happy"
- "I AM well compensated"

If you want something you don't have, then add:

- "I AM finding new and perfect clients"
- "I AM well-compensated"
- "I AM respected by my clients, colleagues, and co-workers"
- "I AM a very important key player in my business/company"

You can add "I AM"s for every aspect of your business, relationships, and even your health.

Then, watch what happens. Not only are you raising your energy and vibration to a higher level, which will positively impact everyone around you, you will positively impact yourself and your results. This process will make you feel amazing. *Trust me on this.* Now stand back and watch the magic happen.

> *"Your words become your life. Choose each one of them wisely."* ~Honorée Corder

Chapter Seven:
Who's On Your Bench?

"Your inner circle determines your outer circumstances." ~Honorée Corder

The great Jim Rohn said, *"You are the average of the five people you spend the most time with."* Mr. Rohn's words are powerful, and they resonate in my mind when developing relationships, pursuing friendships, even engaging new clients.

While I was putting together the concept for the STMA, I knew one-on-one coaching was, and is, effective and result producing, I knew a program with both one-on-one and group coaching would be incredibly powerful and life-changing. The program was designed to maximize the efforts of six individuals, while simultaneously providing the structure for individual and group success. A small but powerful group of individuals holding each other accountable, providing support, encouragement, accountability, referrals and introductions can accelerate results and increase productivity like nothing I've ever seen.

The STMA is representative of a "microcosm of the macrocosm." A coaching group, Bible study, or a group of your closest colleagues is but a small representation of our overall lives, and who we have on our bench, as in who is in our intimate circle, as well as in our inner circles, *matters*. Just as studies show we are much more productive when working in a clean, organized environment, the same increase in productivity shows up in your life not only without drama but is full of rich, fulfilling and mutually-beneficial relationships.

Choosing the people to put on your bench, also known as your teams in life and business, is critical for your success. The key players who stand next to you and those who cheer you on from the stands must be chosen with care and thought. While they are creating their own vision and goals, they are also there to support you in your growth and in the pursuit of your goals and vision … just as you will do for them.

As you have begun to think bigger thoughts and dream bigger dreams, as you put together your 100-Day Plan, so too must you begin to analyze, cull, eliminate, and add to those who form your bench.

I feel fortunate that in the three years I have lived in Austin, I have met some of *the coolest people.* Austin's reputation is unmatched by almost any other city. When we decided to move to Austin, to a person, I heard, "Austin is a terrific city! You will love it! I wish I could live there." Everyone I talked to had either been to Austin and loved it, went to school in Austin, or had heard amazing things about it. *To a person.* It was no surprise to me when I moved here and met some of the people that make up this great city. After spending the better part of a decade in Las Vegas, I had built some close relationships. I knew I would miss my friends, and as a believer in the power of relationships, I intended to find the same type of people here.

I've met probably close to two thousand people. I networked *a lot* for about the first six months, and then began to realize who were my "PLUs." PLU stands for "People Like Us." My group of peeps in Austin is constantly making introductions to other people we meet, and the subject line of the email or text includes, "he's a PLU," meaning, I like him, and if I like him, so will you.

I have a belief that in life you are best surrounded by people who are like you, "your people," a.k.a. PLUs. Some people will like you. Some people won't like you. *That is okay.* Some people will be your people, and you will resonate with them from the first minute you meet. To find as many of your PLUs as possible, you have to sort and keep sorting, because you will probably meet a dozen or even a hundred who aren't PLUs for the one that you do.

If you have a strong network of individuals, a big group of PLUs, who cheer you on in your pursuit of the next level, good for you! More often than not, however, as we grow and expand in our lives and careers, we develop new relationships while others fade away. You may know your bench needs some adjustment, pruning or enhancement, and there's no day like today to begin the process of sorting through a new batch of people until you find the ones who will help you make your vision your reality.

Unlike the bigger network we develop to build our businesses and careers, your bench will most likely consist of a dozen or less. Take a look at your closest friendships, relationships and connections and ask yourself some of these revealing questions:

1. What are the characteristics I need in a close relationship? i.e., has integrity, positive, cheerful, focused, successful, supportive, etc.
2. Who do I know I need to know better?
3. Who would be the best addition to my bench?

Building Your Business Bench: A Sneak Peak at the 12x12 System™

Just as your personal bench consists of close friends, your spouse, and family, your business bench consists of your strategic partners, other valuable contacts, resources, centers of influence, and prospective clients. With a deep bench, you will never be lacking in sweet-spot work, and the possibilities are endless. I have discovered that most professionals have no idea how to identify logical contacts to grow and expand their practices and businesses intentionally.

As part of the 1-on-1 or Group STMA, you are provided with multiple tools to help you get and stay, on track with your marketing and networking efforts. The 12x12 System™ is one tool provided as part of the program to help you organize and build out your business bench to ensure you continue to sustain the momentum you gain in the initial stages.

The 12x12 System™

The 12x12 System™ is a professional's guide to business networking gold. This step-by-step process will help you to create a viable and enviable network, even if you have never networked before, are new to your profession, are shy or hesitant about networking, or all of the above.

Most professionals network in a haphazard and disorganized manner that creates random and hit-or-miss results. It's time to get strategic and intentional about your networking. It's time to do the actions that get the results you desire.

The 12x12 System™ will help you to:

1. Organize your network.
2. Discover "holes" in your network.
3. Get intentional and strategic about connecting with the right Strategic Partners and Centers of Influence.
4. Work smarter, not harder because you have a steady stream of referrals coming to you.
5. Use your networking time more effectively.

The 12x12 System™ Phases

Phase I – Get Organized

1. Determine your professional categories. *What professionals have been the best at sending you your best clients? Write down those categories, put them into your 12x12 columns.*
2. Fill in the connections you already have. *You already know some of these professionals, include them in your 12x12.*
3. Sort categories in order of "importance" (i.e., what categories are *most likely* to send you business first and regularly. Put the

81

"most likely" in the far left graduating to the "least likely" in column twelve.)

Phase II – Get Intentional

4. Identify the most important categories of professionals in which you do not have 12 contacts.

5. Find more professionals. *I suggest searching for and connecting with those professionals 3 ways: through current clients, through others in the same professional category, and through LinkedIn.*

Phase III – Get Going

6. Network, network, network. *Until your 12x12 consists of 144 individuals who refer you business between 1-100 times a year, keep adding, deleting, and refining your network.*

Here is an example of the 12x12 System Grid™:

12 x 12 Matrix System™   Name: _____

In order from left to right (from "most likely" to "least likely" to refer you business), customize your columns. Categories include: Corporate Attorney, Estate Attorney, Tax Attorney, Criminal Attorney, Banker, Investment Banker, Realtor, Commercial Realtor, Insurance Provider, CPA (Audit), CPA (Tax), Financial Advisor, Other/Misc.

	Corp Attorney	Estate Attorney	Tax Attorney	Investment Banker	REALTORS*	Ins. Providers	CPAs	Banker	Mortgage Brokers	Financial Advisors	Consultants	Misc
1												
2												
3												
4												
5												
6												
7												
8												
9												
10												
11												
12												

Insert "Other" for your professional category.

Note: You get access to the complete 12x12 System™ as part of your STMA, should you choose to participate in the 1-on-1 or Group version.

Additional Thoughts

Never ask someone for connections or introductions when you've only just connected with them, unless you have instant rapport (you feel like you've met your long-lost best friend). Just like in personal relationship development, everything takes time ... and we just don't know how long it's going to take before the relationship hits the tipping point.

Networking intentionally, including using the 12x12 System™, works when you work it. The more time you dedicate to it, the faster and better it will work. If you hate networking, are more reserved or shy, or are just getting started, just take it one day at a time. Using a System, like the 12x12 System™, has worked with the most personally challenged professionals and out-going seasoned professionals alike, and *all of them* report actually enjoying the process once they got the hang of it. Rome wasn't built in a day, and developing your network is a career-long process. Just keep making regular progress, and soon you will bear the fruit of your labor.

"You will become just like the people you hang around with, so hang around people who are or are becoming who you aspire to become." ~Honorée Corder

Chapter Eight:
Old Habits Eat Good Intentions
For Lunch

"Your good habits will override any blocks, delays or denials." ~Honorée Corder

Your habits determine your life. Most of us exercise habits we're not even aware of and make decisions based upon the habits we observe in others that they're not even aware of. Not an ideal way of living productively, for sure.

When habits are running our lives that means we are acting, choosing, and living unconsciously. As we have previously discussed, you can choose to develop habits that serve you automatically and help you to unconsciously create almost what you want in your life and business.

Up to this point, you most likely haven't identified the daily activities and actions you desire to turn into habits. You've read this far into this book, which means you might even be thinking, "I'm ready to go. No old habits could possibly stop me."

Danger!

The old habits you have developed, on purpose or by default, have taken you where you are today. You acquired them unconsciously. You acquired them because you observed someone else and picked up their habits. You established some of

85

your habits even as a result of your *other* habits, like getting up for work at a certain time each day and not eating breakfast because you're too rushed, or drinking a cup of coffee mid-afternoon because you ate too many carbs at lunch or didn't get enough rest because you stayed up too late. Much of your behavior is guided by unconscious habits you did not choose, and your life right now is the result of those unconscious choices and habits. Sounds great, right? Not so much.

The danger is that if you continue on your present course, you will end up arriving at the destination you're headed toward right now. I recognize that might not be a bad thing at all, but is your current destination exactly where you want to go, or is it time for some intentional course correction?

I'm going to guess you're not entirely blissed out about the current state of your affairs, or if you are, you have identified there is some additional bliss you would like to experience. Excellent!

You have the option to download a Dashboard and utilize it to ensure you know exactly what to do each day until your chosen actions become your automatic habits. You could intentionally track a few action items to ensure they become habits. Or you could just continue on your present course and hope things work out for you.

Coach's Note: *Hope* is not a business strategy. It's not a personal strategy. Dare I say, and I do, it's not a strategy for any damn thing. Period.

Unless and until you shine your light on the actions and habits that need attention and upgrading, you are under the influence of the habits you already have, habits that could include procrastination, avoidance, or even creating drama or distraction. I think we can agree that some, if not many, of the habits you have right now are simply not going to cut it if you have a major vision that needs to come to fruition.

Willpower is Not Enough

Have you ever *tried* using willpower to break old habits and form new ones? "I can make more money if I just get into the office earlier and make more calls," or "I will use willpower to stop smoking." My personal favorite, "I can keep a bag of chocolate in my freezer and only eat one every night." Nice try.

This attempt at *making* desired results happen through sheer will just doesn't work. As much as we want our commitment to remain strong in spite of obstacles, challenges and waning enthusiasm, it won't.

Here's why:

Willpower is controlled by a part in the brain called the orbital frontal cortex (part of the frontal lobe located in the front of the brain). In order for the orbital frontal cortex to be turned on, it requires an "active focus." You're thinking, "I can actively focus." Maybe, maybe not. Let me explain.

If I say to you, "Don't think of a pink elephant," what are you most likely to do? You will, of course, think of a pink elephant. Therefore, each time you think to yourself "Don't eat the chocolate chip cookies," you will constantly think of and want to eat the chocolate chip cookies. Before you know it, you're giving into the chocolate chip cookies and thinking of yourself in a negative manner for not having the willpower to say *"no."*

When you turn off your "active focus," the old habits kick in. You find yourself with the cookie half-eaten and then realize you just set aside an intention not to eat any sugar until you reach your goal weight. Or you know you need to make ten prospective client calls, only to realize at the office on Wednesday you haven't made a single one.

The reason I want you to identify the actions you need to have as habits in order for you to be successful is because I want you to start living toward your vision *on purpose*. I'm giving you a visual accountability tool to make sure your chosen actions get done consistently, and turn into habits that will effortlessly propel you forward toward your vision's creation. I'm not just speaking in terms of the STMA because I want you to be massively successful in your overall life, and I know that won't happen unless you have the right habits. I also know how tough old habits are to overcome, especially if you don't have the right structure to make your goals a reality.

Know this: you have within you the power to choose, and you have at your fingertips the structure to make what you've chosen a reality.

Engineering Circumstances

Committing to specific actions long enough to turn them into habits means you have to engineer circumstances to support you, in spite of anything and everything ... including you. Engineering circumstances means you put systems, rituals, rules and/or intentions in place to thwart you in the event you try to procrastinate, delay or even fail to perform the tasks you know would ensure your success.

While it's nearly impossible to force yourself to follow through, there are four effective techniques you can use to engineer circumstances for ensuring that before long, you automatically execute what you know would be in your best interest. We've determined the Six Daily Actions that should become your Six Daily Habits to be: *Your AM Routine, Rainmaking, Work Product, Keeping Current Clients Happy, Admin,* and *Personal Time with Friends and Family.* Let's engineer some circumstances around turning those Actions into Habits:

1. **Right before wrong.** Let's suppose you've chosen to lose weight as part of your 100 Days. Right out of the gate, you eat steamed broccoli with grilled chicken for lunch and dinner and walk 10,000 steps a day. For the first few days, this is easy because your resolve is strong and your willpower still firmly intact. But by about day 6, your wife makes "the best pancakes on Earth" for Sunday brunch, and the smell of the pancakes combined with the aroma of bacon and eggs leaves your previous restraint a distant memory. Soon you're licking the plate clean, only to realize you've fallen off your Program without any awareness.

   Enter *Right before wrong.* By thinking back on times when you've indulged or procrastinated in the past, you can write some new rules and intentions to foil any situation that confronts you that might even possibly take you off track.

My personal rules include: *I can eat whatever I want, but I have to walk at least 10,000 steps a day,* and *I can enjoy television in the evening as long as I've done my Miracle Morning,* and *I can buy whatever I want as long as I've saved at least 10% of my income and all of my bills are paid.*

Back to the pancakes: your personal rule could be, *I can eat the pancakes, bacon and eggs and enjoy every delicious bite but I've got to spend an hour in the gym first {or within a hour after eating}.*

2. **Create compelling reasons.** While there may be no question as to why a particular action should become a habit, sometimes there has to be a clear reward or a dire consequence to get us to follow through, all the way through. Once you're able to pay your bills, have some money saved and invested, and are able to take vacations a few times a year, the urgency you felt in your early career days may be, well, less urgent. This is where **Create compelling reasons** comes into play.

I recently went through a major downsizing, or actually "right-sizing" in my personal life. After following the social dictum of "accumulate money and things" for the first twenty-five years of my adult life, I realized I no longer owned my things. My things were actually owning me, and I wasn't enjoying it like I thought I would. I didn't like moving them, cleaning them, organizing them, or even having them. As a family we gave away, donated or threw away about 80% of our belongings. We moved into a smaller place, which has more benefits than I could list here, and as a side note, has been one of the best things I have ever done.

The process of right-sizing now causes thought to go into purchasing new items. My new mantra is *experiences over things* as I much prefer enjoying a nice meal at a restaurant with a bunch of friends, or traveling and exploring a new city, over buying new clothes or tchotchkes. My rules around buying things are: *I can buy one thing, but I must get rid of one thing,* and *I can spend money on this vacation, just as soon I get a new institutional client or sell X number of books.* The first provides a consequence, the second a reward. These rules create compelling reasons around my actions, and cause forethought and intention to come into play automatically.

You, too, can write rules to keep yourself on track, such as *I can leave by 3 pm on Friday if I've originated a new matter this week,* or *I must not leave the office until it is completely clean and organized,* or *I can take a 3 day weekend but first I must bill X number of hours.*

3. **Lead a horse to water.** Sometimes all we need is the tiniest of incentives, a mini "priming of

the pump," to get things started. Tony Robbins is quoted as saying, *"Emotion is created by motion."* I know I used to wake up every day, before reading *The Miracle Morning*, and argue with myself while getting ready to hop on the treadmill. I didn't want to workout, yet I knew I would feel great all day if I did. I literally would be putting on my shoes and saying to myself, *"I don't need to go today. I'm already fit. I'm tired and could use an extra hour of sleep."*

I instituted a personal rule years ago, *"I never press the snooze button,"* and *"If I work out for five minutes and I'm still miserable, then I can stop and go get in the shower."* You know what? Not one time have I ever just worked out for only five minutes. As soon as I get on the machine and hear the first song of my workout playlist, the workout mood overtakes me and I complete each and every workout ... and get to enjoy the endorphins that follow! To this day, I live by those two rules, and my alarm goes off at 4:30 a.m. every day, including weekends. I don't always love getting up, but once I'm up, I enjoy the major progress I make on my goals every day. So will you.

When I have something to clean, I'll set the timer for fifteen minutes and just *start*. I'll either listen to music or an audiobook. By the time I hear the timer going off, I'm already in the zone and excited to get the job finished, so I just keep at it.

When you have an action you don't want to complete, give yourself a finite period of time to work on it or do it, and if you still aren't able to get engaged, schedule another time to get it done later in the day or the next day. Most of the time, however, you will find yourself knee-deep in the task and have it done before you know it.

4. **Going too far.** When all else fails, sometimes you just have to go big or go home. And I mean literally "go home." Seriously, sometimes you've got to overdo something in order to shock yourself into actually doing what you really need and want to get done. Yes, I will explain.

A client called me this morning and explained he had just completed two weeks of massive action and had achieved major results. But when he woke up on Monday morning, all of his motivation *was gone*. He didn't want to check the boxes on his Dashboard. He didn't want to follow up with prospective clients. Heck, he didn't want to do anything at all! He's in the midst of his first STMA, so he called because he recognized he'd been in this position before: mentally and physically worn out, and still very aware there was much to do. Concerned he was self-sabotaging, he wanted to know how to avoid losing the momentum he's spent the last two months building.

I made several suggestions: calendar time off at regular intervals. Use the above strategies to ensure he was at least minimally productive, even if he chose to take the majority of a day off, and, *when all else failed*, to allow himself to literally do nothing. For the entire day. No calls, emails, meetings, productive work. I encouraged him to take the day off in a big way. Watch an entire series on Netflix. Take a shower and put on new pajamas. Have food delivered. And finally, put a time limit on this very awesome and incredibly effective indulgence. Take the entire day off, but get up at 4 a.m. the next morning and get back after it in a new way.

Going too far can also be effective with your diet. In *The Four Hour Body*, Tim Ferriss advises to eat according to very strict guidelines six days a week. On the seventh day, you eat whatever you want, as much as you want, to satiate your inner beast. I know it works because I do it and I've been able to lose weight by eating myself into oblivion one day a week and eating and exercising to optimal potential during the rest of the week. If you find yourself dying for a piece of cheesecake on Tuesday, but your free day is Saturday, eat the cheesecake. As in, eat the whole cheesecake! You probably will end up nauseous and never, ever want to eat cheesecake again, and you won't want anything else that isn't green and good for you for at least a few days. Mission accomplished!

As we've discussed before, you can have the best of intentions when it comes to your goals and success.

You can intend to check all of your boxes, follow through like an overachieving super freak, but when you lose your drive, use the above strategies to ensure you keep making progress no matter what.

All of the above engineering of circumstances will help you to turn your actions into habits quickly and easily. Schedule some time to thoughtfully write your rules and intentions and begin to engineer your circumstances, and therefore your success. I suggest *now*.

"Bad habits cause immediate benefit but long-term harm. Good habits cause immediate benefit and long-term benefit. Develop habits that positively serve you long-term." ~Honorée Corder

Chapter Nine:
PLAN: Prepare, Launch, Accountability, Next!

"If you are not able to see your goals, they will take longer to achieve, and sometimes "longer" is "never." ~Honorée Corder

You've read this far, and that means to me you're a person committed to their personal and professional development. Not one to settle, you're truly ready for the next level. Well, I have something that can make leaping to the next level seem like a tiny, effortless jump.

The STMA coaching program was born from my desire to be improving constantly and achieving the next level and along with that, bigger and better goals. I wanted a way to track my progress easily and to improve my performance continually.

Because I didn't (don't) prefer complex math, I decided to work in 100-day increments. Calendar quarters range in number from 88 to 92 days. In order to figure out where I was percent-to-goal, there was a whole lot of multiplying and dividing going on, and yes, that would be math.

Working in 100-day increments means that each day is 1% of goal. Easy! For example, a goal of $100,000 could be divided equally and effortlessly tracked: 1% per day equals $1,000 per day. Either I was ahead, on track, or behind my goals based upon how many percentage points I had on a given day. On day 57, I should be at 57% to goal (or higher) or $57,000. Or, I'm behind and I know I need to catch up, and exactly how much I need to catch up. I always know right where I am and where I should be. It is easy to tell right where I am in relation to my goal – without the math.

The basis of the STMA is the PLAN you put in place prior to your Day 1 start, or frankly the start of any goal-achievement odyssey.

Your Plan consists of several important pieces:

> **Dates:** These are the dates of your 100 days. For example, Day 1 is January 1, 2013 through Day 100, April 10, 2013.

> **100-Day Vision:** This is your "what." What do you want to accomplish, bring to fruition, and achieve over the next 100 days? Visualize it and then describe it with total certainty and positive expectation.

> **100-Day Purpose:** This is your "why." What would accomplishing your "what" give you, provide for you, help you to achieve down the road?

> **Top 3 Goals:** The 3 most important things you wish to accomplish during your STMA™. Make them SMART: Specific, Measurable, Attainable, Risky (at least a little) , and Time-sensitive. The deadline for these goals is, of course, your 100th Day.

> **Empowering Descriptors:** This is the fun part of the serious business of goal-achievement. Give yourself a reputation to

live up to. Use phrases that help you to turn on and rev up. My empowering descriptors include: Marketing Master! Queen of Manifestation! Best Mom Ever!

Three Areas of Focus: These are the three areas of your business and life you want to focus on during the Program. They could include marketing, advertising, weight loss (or gain), positioning, client development, recruiting, etc.

Resources: These are the people (including us, your virtual and literal coaches) and things you can rely on to shorten your success cycle. They could include books, seminars, music, mentors, CD programs, bosses, friends, and family.

Next Steps: This is your "data dump." Get out of your head and on paper every single thing that needs to get done, regardless of whether or not it (a) has anything to do with your STMA™ and (b) has to be done by you (or right now you think it does). These items could include the people you need to call, proposals that need follow-up, cleaning out your car, buying cat food, or sending a card to your mom. If you're carrying it around in your head, it's adding to your stress level and making you less effective. Take your list and put the items in order of importance. Your items will fall into one of four categories: *Do, Delegate, Delay,* or *Dump.* There is no limit to the amount of items that go on this list. You will add to it over time, but as you add items, be sure to categorize them and treat them as appropriate.

PREPARE

Preparation is key in any endeavor, and the STMA is no exception.

"Proper preparation prevents particularly poor performance." ~ *The 6 P's Principle*

A big part of being successful, and having a successful 100-Days, is taking the time to do the pre-work necessary, including answering some tough questions that reveal potential areas of focus, getting organized, and making sure you're ready to go. Rest assured that the STMA is designed to help you "shore up" any areas that need attention, so don't worry too much if what you discover through your preparation is that you're really just not prepared. You'll get there, just stay the course and stay focused and determined.

Here is the definition of STMA, the Steps you will go through as you progress through the Program, and the psychological stages you'll most likely experience.

First, let's define **STMA™** and what purpose it will serve for you and your business. Again, **STMA™** stands for *"Short-Term Massive Action™."*

Engaging in the STMA™ will help you to:

1. Identify your Point A (where you are now) and your Point B (where you want to go and the results you want to create).

2. Step up your level of *intensity, intention, attention to detail,* and *sense of urgency.*

3. Work smarter, not harder.

4. Create *unstoppable momentum, more life balance, more business,* and *more money* than ever before (and more than you ever thought possible!).

5. Get and stay on track.

6. Maintain integrity, balance, and fulfillment.

7. Be the difference between mediocre and fabulous!

8. All of the above becomes your Plan A.

The Steps

These are the Program steps you will work through and will keep you focused and moving forward through your coaching sessions.

> **Step 1: Prepare and Create Your 100-Day Action Plan.** This Step includes completing the Pre-Start Checklist, answering the Pre-Launch Questions, and completing the on-boarding with your group coach.
>
> **Step 2: Set Yourself Up for Success: Put Systems in Place to Speed Up Your Success.** There is a System for everything, including goal-achievement and success. This system will include the additional tools in the Program, such as a couple recommended in this book: *The Miracle Morning book* and *The 12x12 System™.* Others could include a contact management system or hiring an assistant, office manager, business development officer, or even a housekeeper. You will uncover and

discover those needs during the question-answering phase and during your individual, group or self-study coaching sessions.

Step 3: Support and Sabotage. Anticipating Pushback, Preparing to Avoid Naysayers, and Overcoming Distractions and Detours. If someone isn't supporting you, they might be sabotaging you. Be sure those you have around you encourage, inspire, and motivate you to continue to move to the next level. We recommend you surround yourself with other awesome folks, you could even find others to do the STMA with you.

Step 4: Think It. Feel It. Know It. Own it! As you progress through the STMA, you will discover just what is possible for you to achieve when you focus. Focus was the subject of a coach call I had with a CPA yesterday. He said, "I can't believe how much I'm able to get done when I'm intentional and purposeful." I encourage you to become *ruthlessly discriminating* and *intentional and purposeful* about how you spend your minutes, just as you spend your dollars. As you become more aware, you automatically build your self-confidence muscle. Your true abilities, which may have remained undiscovered or dormant for years, come to light. You will soon *own your greatness*.

Step 5: Creating Your Team: The Power of Your Environment. Your team consists of your spouse or significant other, your closest friends, your strategic partners, and your personal and professional advisors. *Choose them wisely, for they determine just how successful you will become.*

The Stages

You can expect to go through each of these Stages. As your coach, I *expect* you to do whatever is necessary to keep your mind right, such as listen to the audios about attitude and self-talk, reach out to your coach, or read a book on attitude, when you feel like staying focused and intentional is getting "tough." I have shared with you the skills that will help you to shift your self-talk within a matter of moments so you can get back to the most important thing: moving forward.

Stage 1: Excitement ... "I'm ready!" Feeling excited and energized is normal at the very beginning of anything, from marriage to a new weight loss program. This initial enthusiasm lasts from two to six weeks, depending upon your commitment to the outcomes you have decided upon and the results you may see right away.

Stage 2: Frustration ... "Is my coach crazy? There's so much to do, so little time!" Before you've mastered the skills of organization and having purposeful intention, you may feel overwhelmed with all there is to do. I know the feeling! Take a deep breath and do what you can while you notice what's working and not working.

There's a tip, tool, system, or strategy for that (but, alas, so sorry, no app).

Stage 3: Overwhelmed ... "Maybe I am unable to do it all." As you trust the process and engage your newfound skills, you will realize many things about yourself, and one of them will be how much can be accomplished in a day, week, month, and 100-days. I promise.

Stage 4: Ah Ha! ... "I can do it!" This is a fun stage, I won't lie. Once you realize letting go of the stories about why you can't do something, scheduling time for each activity that's truly important and crossing it off, and actually make measurable progress, you'll realize just how unstoppable you truly are.

Stage 5: Pride ... "I did it!" On your 100th day, you'll look back and marvel at all you've been able to accomplish. One day, one checked box at a time.

Pre-STMA™ Checklist: Get Yourself Ready

Before you can run, you must walk, before you walk, you must crawl, and to the best of my knowledge, rolling over precedes crawling. So, along that line, let's cover the basics and get you set up for success!!

Here's your pre-start checklist. Prior to launching your first 100 Days, you must have completed the following six items:

☐   I have completed my 100-Day Action Plan and, if appropriate, sent it to my coach.

☐   I have identified my Point A by answering the Pre-STMA™ Questions and, if appropriate, sent them to my coach.

☐   I have a fabulous attitude, and I'm ready for massive momentum, big changes, and new opportunities!

☐   I have purchased a Moleskine notebook, journal, or an iPad notebook app to use for the Program.

☐   I have a tool to use as my calendar, to hold my database of contacts, etc. (Outlook, an iPhone, BlackBerry, or Franklin-Covey Planner).

Pre-STMA™ Questions: Where are You Now?

These are the questions you'll want to contemplate and complete prior to your Day 1.[2]

Defining your Point A (where you are now) and discovering your Point B (where you want to go). The most important part of creating the life and business you desire is to take an inventory of where you are right now, what needs to be addressed, and what you want to create in the future, specifically the near-future … the next 100-days! Calendar two hours to ponder and complete these questions.

---

[2] These questions and all of the documents you need are included in your on-boarding documents, should you choose to participate in any version of the STMA.

Why are you here?

Describe everything you would like to have in your life now.

What would you attempt do if you were certain you would achieve success?

Where am I now?

Describe your life now (home environment, hobbies, vacations, relationship status, etc.).

Describe your business now (numbers, income, number and type of clients, etc.).

List the accomplishments, personally and professionally, you are most proud about.

What's working?

Based on your current results, describe what is and has been working in your life.

Based on your current results, describe what is and has been working in your career.

What's not working?

What activities are you currently doing (life/career) that could be delegated, and who could do them?

Describe your biggest time wasters (email, phone calls, co-workers, housework, etc.).

What do you need to let go of or stop doing?

What else is not working?

Moving Forward

Describe what you would like your **life** to look like within 100 days.

Describe what you would like your **business** to look like within 100 days.

Based on what you described above, share your level of commitment to making these desires a reality.

What needs to be in place for you to get your **life** in the best place to move forward?

What needs to be in place for you to get your **business** in the best place to move forward?

What do you want more of?

How specifically can your coach/mentor/boss/advisors support you?

Should you fail to complete the assignments/tasks/activities from the Program, what are the consequences you would encounter?

LAUNCH

Once you've completed your pre-Start questions, completed your pre-Start checklist, and perhaps identified your fellow team-members (or they've been identified for you), partner in success or decided to go it alone, you are ready to launch. Your official launch date is your Day 1.

The Program has been designed to keep you focused and making progress long after the mood to commit to the Program has left you. I understand you're going to lose your initial enthusiasm. You are going to encounter challenges, illness, setbacks, and delays. The Program works when you work it, I promise. The structure is such that if you show up and keep showing up or begin showing up sooner (after you've encountered one of the afore-mentioned challenges), you will make measurable progress. You will move closer to your goals and objectives. You will build your "achiever muscles." How am I so sure? In a word: accountability.

ACCOUNTABILITY

As I've mentioned before, when you don't have some form of accountability, you will let yourself slide. You will give yourself an extra day, week, month, year, five years, or even a decade to achieve something. Time passes, and it passes quickly. Eventually, you look up and realize if you had just started when you first thought about it, you would have finished that degree, grown that company, or achieved that goal. If you have even one point of accountability, it can increase your chances of achievement immeasurably. But I don't want to increase your chances. *I virtually want to ensure them.* The STMA provides exactly the kind of accountability you need.

My Five Points of Accountability System™

1. **You {the Participant}:** You are accountable to yourself. You wouldn't be interested in the STMA if you didn't want something more in your career and your life.

2. **Cash:** The STMA, in the form of this Program in any format or even this book, costs money. You had to earn the money to pay for it, or you had to convince someone to pay for you. Whether it was your boss and the company or you and your family who paid for you, I know you want to get value

108

for the money that was paid. You don't just pay out your cold hard cash for something you don't intend to take full advantage of, do you? I know businesses and spouses surely don't, so they will be checking in and holding you accountable for those dollars spent.

3. **The Coaches**: In the Group Coaching Program, you have two coaches, or one coach who plays two roles: the Group Coach and the Individual Coach. The Group Coach provides the One-on-One Pre-Start Strategy Session with each participant in order to enable each client to crystallize his or her initial vision, choose three concrete goals, move strategically chosen daily actions into habits, and utilize other strategies that will enable them to achieve their goals. There are twenty-seven (27) Group Coach-Facilitated, 15-25 minute group-coaching sessions. Each participant receives three 50-minute customized coaching calls. Working closely with the Group Coach to maximize each call, these sessions are held around weeks 4, 8, and 12 of the Program. Also provided are three separate tools to maximize each participant's progress. If you are your coach, you'll want to be sure to read and re-read Chapter 8 until you've mastered the techniques for engineering circumstances.

4. **Peer Accountability & Strategic Partner Engagement**: In any version of the STMA, you will be working with your buddy or fellow group members to strategize ways to

network, to give and receive referrals, and to stay on track.

5. **The STMA Dashboard:** The STMA Dashboard is a Strategic Planning tool used as a guiding star to ensure maximum productivity and progress. The Dashboard allows for accountability to be transparent to both coaches and participant. Here's a snapshot of the Dashboard, and you can download a complimentary copy here: **http://tinyurl.com/STMADASHBOARD.**

NEXT!

You're off on your new adventure, and I know you're so excited. The anticipation is high, and frankly your expectations are too, right? In the next 100 days, you will meet new people, make authentic connections, grow yourself, your business and career, and begin what will in essence be your new life.

You are probably also a tad nervous and apprehensive, which is to be expected. Over the years I've heard:

1) *"How will I know if I do it right?"* There is no right or wrong; instead, there's effective and ineffective. You will learn what you're doing that's effective, and you'll also learn what's ineffective and have a chance to make adjustments. We're not looking for perfection here; we're looking for progress.

2) *"What if I get to the end, and I've failed to achieve my goals?"* You have not failed if you've made some kind of progress, and you've learned something. Truthfully, 100-days is an artificial deadline that's been set for measurement purposes only. Nothing bad happens on the 100th day if you don't achieve your goals. No one is losing his or her birthdays here, ladies and gentlemen. Most do achieve their goals or at least make measureable progress, and everyone agrees they learn valuable lessons about themselves and their businesses. They also agree they learned where they could focus more intensely, be more intentional in their efforts, be more purposeful in their actions, and learn to enjoy the journey even more.

3) *"I hated answering those questions; I felt horrible about what they revealed."* Put down the hammer and stop being so hard on yourself! What or who does that serve? You are your harshest critic, but criticism without understanding or insight is not valuable. What would be more effective would be to recognize where you have been ineffective in the past, and resolve to make a concerted effort to change consistently what needs

111

changing over time. Some of that time is right now, during the next 100-days.

Let's change the focus and get clear about what you are anticipating. Are you anticipating that great things are going to happen in your life and business over the next 100 days? Are you looking forward to meeting new and potential clients, and are, therefore, taking purposeful action to do so? Are you anticipating seeing the results of your efforts this week, next week, next month, and long after this particular 100 days has come to an end?

Part of anticipating is picturing in your mind's eye what you want to happen in the future, (in this case in the next 100 days) *all day, every day,* and no matter what you're actually seeing in your reality right now. Truthfully, what you see with your eyes doesn't matter; what you see in your mind and the pictures you hold there is what really counts. If your business right now is the picture of health and success, you want to make it bigger and better. If your business isn't the picture of health and success, you just want to get it healthy and successful (as you define health and success).

You're in luck; the STMA is here to help you to have a healthy and successful business.

Take a few moments and do this closed-eye exercise: Picture your top three goals and visualize them as being achieved. Feel in your body the emotions you will feel – excited, thrilled, awesome-sauce -- when they have actually been achieved. Create a sense of anticipation; the side benefit will be that you will take action when times are tough, when you get a "no" instead of a "yes," or it even seems like what you're striving for might not happen (it will, or something even better will).

Now you have a movie you can play in your mind as many times a day as you need it, on demand! Any time you feel unsure, full of doubt or even fearful you won't achieve your goals, just close your eyes and play your movie. Be sure to work this into your daily goal-achievement practices ... stay in bed just five extra minutes to "watch your movie" and be sure to have a nightly screening just before you head off to dreamland. That anticipation you have created will be recreated and sustained and thus will be really powerful, and I know if you harness that power, you'll be just as excited about what's coming up next in your life as I am in mine!

"Massive action is the father of achievement."
~Honorée Corder

Chapter Ten:
Now Get What You Really Want

*"Be the one to turn your wishes, desires, and wants
into actions, plans and results. Start today.
You deserve it." ~Honorée Corder*

You are exceptional because you have gotten to this point. Ninety percent of all books, programs, and plans go uncompleted for many of the reasons I've discussed in *Vision to Reality*. Now that you have an understanding of the philosophy of the STMA, it's up to you to do the work to turn *your vision* into *your reality*.

My mastermind partner started with weekly updates at the beginning of 2013. He said, "I've started doing weekly updates before, where I measured my metrics and then eventually got off track. Not this time." He was determined not to drop the ball, and he didn't for a really long time … until he got off track because he got a promotion and started traveling a lot more. As a group, we got him right back on track. He knew he needed to check the boxes, and he thought about checking the boxes, but he didn't check the boxes. It wasn't until he recommitted to his vision that he got right back in the game.

As we have discussed, you will get off track. Yes, it can happen to you. While it is impossible to avoid the occasional bump in the road, the decision remains yours as to how you will handle it when the time comes.

Getting what you want, creating your vision, is absolutely possible. You now must make the decision that achieving your vision is more important than anything else. Then you create the awesome, rock-solid, and inspiring plan to ensure it becomes your reality.

I believe in making things as simple as possible, and along those lines, I'm providing a road map of next steps so in the very near future you will be actually living your vision. Your vision will have become your reality, and by then you will be plotting and visualizing a brand new, bigger vision. The program is very simple, but it's not easy. Are you ready? Let's go!

The STMA and Your Success

Step 1: Choose or engage in the STMA Program that works best for you: self-study, company-sponsored, strategic partners or individual audio program. Contact Honorée Enterprises at info@CoachHonoree.com or 512-578-9807.

Step 2: Do the STMA pre-work, and if you're a part of a live group, schedule on-boarding with your group coach.

Step 3: Work the program every single day for 100 days.

Step 4: Celebrate your success.

Step 5: Repeat.

Now, go make yourself proud by envisioning your future, setting some powerful goals, putting a solid plan in place, and taking action until you've achieved everything on your list.

What Now?

You rock: you've read all the way to this point. You're clearly ready to make some changes in your life and career. If you weren't a special being, you would have read only the first chapter, or you'd still be meaning to start this book.

It's time for you to stop reading and start doing. Take wishing and hoping right out of your vocabulary, commit to yourself and your dreams, and take action.

You can continue to hope the right time to begin will come along, and here's the God's honest truth: you're going to be hoping for a long, long time. Let me say this again: *hope* is not a strategy for anything. Wishing won't make anything happen, either. Commitment, planning, and action are the cornerstones of achievement.

You want a better life. To make more money. Have better relationships. Be more productive. Go more places. I know you do. What are you going to do about it *today?*

It's up to you to take the reins of your life and craft and sculpt your life, relationships, self and career into exactly what you want.

Coach's Challenge: Get coaching.

Engaging a coach to hold you accountable, use as a sounding board, strategize your best next steps, and help you talk through decisions will change your life for the better. Pick the STMA program that works best for you, craft your 100-day Plan and then take your progress one day at a time.

I absolutely guarantee you will be glad you did.

"It's time. Go!" ~Honorée Corder

STMA Options

Options, Choices, and Opportunities

You have multiple ways to engage in an STMA 100-Day Program: on your own, the STMA Audio, individual 1-on-1 coaching with a Certified STMA Coach, or in a group of six.

On Your Own

Take the structure and tools found in this book, set your day one, and do your pre-work. Many people have successfully completed their 100-days and lived to tell the tale.

I'm not a hard-core salesperson, but I would be remiss if I didn't point out that having some form of accountability drastically increases one's chances of success. At the very least, get yourself a buddy and put in place some dire consequences if you don't follow through.

The STMA Audio

Wanting coaching and being in a place to afford coaching sometimes are two entirely different places. As my Certified STMA Coach Wendy Nolin said to me when she hired me, "I can't afford to hire you, so I can't afford not to hire you."

Our least expensive, and still very effective version of STMA, is the STMA Audio Program.

The Audio Program consists of twenty-seven (27) audio coaching sessions with my Certified Coach Extraordinaire Joan Richardson and me discussing topics to keep you on track in the same format as the live groups, such as attitude, time maximization, organization, developing strategic partners, and networking.

You'll listen to the audios based on the structure of the Program, and dare I say, you'll have a fine time doing it, while creating the results you want.

STMA Group Coaching

As I mentioned earlier, going through a coaching process with others, strategically chosen others, can be a fun and rewarding process. The Group option brings you together with five other individuals who are either within your company at the same level, or are strategic partners chosen because you can, in addition to holding each other accountable, refer each other business. A win-win-win!

STMA Individual 1-on-1 Coaching

When you know you can't or won't complete a successful 100-days on your own, you're not a group participation type of person, or you want the level of coaching, accountability, and results that only 1-on-1 coaching can provide, this could be the option for you.

You can get information on any of these options by reaching out to my office at 512-578-9807. Yes, I'm standing by and waiting for your call!

Gratitude

My life works because I'm surrounded by the best people. This book got done because I had the love and support of some pretty crazy-amazing people!

To my husband, partner and best friend Byron, you've upped my cool factor by a lot. Thank you for everything you bring to my life. I love you.

To my daughter and inspiration, Lexi, I'm so grateful to be your mom. Thank you for being so awesome! I love you.

To my bestie, back-up singer and shoe-shopping partner, Joan, you're just the greatest. I love having you to work with, play with, and shop with.

To my mastermind peeps, Rich, Andrea, Scott, and Jerald ~ there are no words. I'm so grateful for our synergy.

To you! *Are you still here?* Then you for sure are going to want to call my office at 512-578-9807 and get started turning your vision into your reality with the right STMA Program for you ... today!

Who is Honorée

Honorée Corder is a Best-selling Author, Speaker, and Executive Coach, helping her clients grow their businesses and live amazing lives. She empowers others to dream big and go for what they truly want.

Author. Honorée is the author of *The Successful Single Mom* book series, *The Successful Single Dad*, *Play2Pay*, *Paying4College,* and *Tall Order!*

Coach. Her ground-breaking STMA (Short-Term-Massive-Action) 100-Day Coaching Program is available for individuals and groups.

Honorée Enterprises, Inc.
Honoree@CoachHonoree.com
http://www.HonoreeCorder.com
http://www.SuccessfulSingleMomBook.com
Twitter: http://www.twitter.com/Honoree
Facebook: http://www.facebook.com/Honoree
Smashwords: http://tinyurl.com/HCCSmashwords
My blog: http://Honoree.blogspot.com